CIR Study 5:

Trade Union Recognition: CIR Experience

London   Her Majesty's Stationery Office 1974

This study was carried out by Bernard James and Edward Pleasance under the direction of Gavril Robertson, Deputy Secretary to the Commission. The authors wish to express their appreciation for the many helpful comments and contributions made by Commissioners and colleagues on the staff of the CIR.

ii

Contents

Preface

This study examines the way in which the Commission on Industrial Relations (CIR) has considered the various issues that have arisen during its handling of trade union recognition cases. A study of this nature will be useful to those who are engaged in handling future recognition claims since it draws attention to the main issues which should receive consideration when negotiating machinery is being established. It is not intended that the study should provide detailed practical guidance on the way in which recognition cases should be handled. The Commission has already published its views and given this kind of guidance in its annual reports. It has also produced a staff study on recognition which is of general application although based on the chemical and engineering industries. It is not the aim of this paper to provide a commentary on the recognition provisions of the Industrial Relations Act.

The study which is based on published CIR reports was originally intended for internal staff purposes. It has been approved for publication by the Commission in the belief that it will be of interest to a wider audience. Those who are interested in the way in which the CIR has carried out its terms of reference in recognition cases and contributed towards the development of public policy in this area will find the paper of particular interest.

1 Introduction

1. This study examines the detailed issues that the CIR has had to consider in its handling of trade union recognition cases. It is based on a close analysis of published CIR reports* which was undertaken to see how the arguments advanced in favour of particular bargaining units and in support of claims to represent employees for full negotiating purposes have been considered by the Commission. The Commission has recommended that unions be granted rights short of full recognition on a number of occasions but these are not considered in detail in this study. Most of the CIR recognition references have concerned claims to represent white-collar employees but the issues examined may arise whenever recognition claims are made.

2. Recognition disputes can give rise to a variety of complex problems when a claim is made by a single union but even more so when more than one organisation is involved. One question that necessarily arises is the group or groups of employees which should be covered by an appropriate negotiating process. These "bargaining unit" problems are often acute since appropriate groupings for bargaining purposes are often difficult to define. Consequently from the start of the Commission's work on recognition cases it has given a great deal of attention to the definition of appropriate bargaining units.

3. There are no clear general principles which can be followed in handling bargaining unit questions. There is no one type of grouping of employees which will be appropriate for all sets of circumstances. For example, an apparently easy solution might be to establish the widest possible units such as company-wide units. However, this might fail to take account of common interest groups within a company which might require separate representation in different units. Conversely an attempt to base bargaining units on narrow occupational groups within a firm may be equally inappropriate since, by neglecting wider common interests, fragmented and unstable bargaining arrangements may result. These and other possible general solutions are therefore inadequate and bargaining units have to be determined in the circumstances of each particular case. For example, while it may be appropriate for some companies to establish company-wide units, in other cases two or more units may be appropriate.

4. When a detailed examination is made of what is likely to be the most appropriate number and extent of bargaining units the investigation is

---

*The reports examined include all those up to CIR Report No. 82

1

largely concerned to discover the nature and extent of the common interest groups among employees. For bargaining units to be stable and viable in the long run they have to be based on the common interests of the employees who are to be covered by collective bargaining. In some cases, separate common interest groups will be capable of supporting bargaining by themselves and may not easily be associated with other groups for bargaining purposes. In others groups may be associated together, possibly in a single company-wide unit, and the unit will then include a number of groups linked together by wider shared common interests.

5. In order to determine what common interest groups are present and whether they can be associated together the factors which give rise to them have to be carefully examined. Broadly such factors relate to the nature of the work group, the pattern of trade union membership and collective representation, and managerial policies and the organisation of the firm. In Chapter 2 we are primarily concerned to examine the factors which led the CIR to make its recommendations on bargaining units in recognition cases.

6. To assist in the examination of the factors which determine the common interests of employees the concept of a "core group" is introduced in Chapter 2. A core group is defined in this study as a group of employees with strong common interests in collective representation around which a possible bargaining unit could be formed. In any particular case it is possible that there will be a number of core groups in the workforce and the boundaries of a bargaining unit might be drawn to include some or all of these groups. Typically, in recognition cases, a spokesman for a group of employees who might also be a trade union representative will approach management and seek recognition to represent employees on an individual or collective basis on issues concerned with their employment. The members of such a core group might have already joined a trade union and they might also have taken some form of action to demonstrate the unity of the group in its claim for recognition. Where the members of a core group have already taken steps to demonstrate their common interests it is much easier to identify it. However, the question concerning the presence of a core group is the first of a number which have to be answered when determining bargaining unit issues. It is also necessary to establish how far the membership of a group extends; to decide whether a single core group could constitute a bargaining unit by itself; and to decide whether two or more core groups could be associated together to constitute a bargaining unit. In practice, the Commission has not approached its work explicitly using this framework. However, a decision about which employees should be members of what units involves one or more of these four questions, and factors are identified to help to answer them.

7. The factors which contribute to the formation of common interests are relevant to all types of bargaining unit issues. Employees in work groups which may form the core of a unit can be identified by the common

2

characteristics of their employment which may give rise to common interests. Any possible extension of a core group beyond its immediately apparent membership will be suggested by the sharing of some common employment characteristics with other employees. Whether an extended core group could or should constitute a unit will depend on the strength of the common interests and the desire for collective representation to which they give rise. Finally, the possible association of core groups into wider units will be suggested by the extent to which interests are shared by different groups, and the strength with which these interests are perceived. Before examining these particular factors in Chapter 2 we consider issues which can arise in the determination of bargaining unit questions.

8. The Commission has taken great care in assessing the relevant factors before making bargaining unit recommendations because of the importance of ensuring that units are appropriate to particular cases. Bargaining units are fundamental to the process of collective bargaining since in return for the right to negotiate with employers a recognised union undertakes to represent the employees in a unit. The precise definition of units is, therefore, of considerable importance for a number of reasons. Included among these reasons are:

(i) a bargaining unit indicates the groups of employees who will be covered by jointly-negotiated terms and conditions of employment;

(ii) a unit enables an employer, employees, a union or unions to know the coverage of any collective agreements that are made;

(iii) a unit delineates the employees on whose behalf a union or unions can be expected to raise individual and collective grievances;

(iv) it delineates the groups of employees among whom a union can be expected to carry out its recruitment and organisational maintenance activities including the appointment and servicing of shop stewards;

(v) it defines the area of employment in which a union can expect to be granted various facilities by management to do its job effectively;

(vi) it defines the groups of employees who will be covered by joint procedural arrangements, e.g. disputes, redundancy, disciplinary and safety procedures;

(vii) it defines the area within which a union or unions will be able to enjoy sole negotiating rights.

9. A bargaining unit then establishes rights of collective representation for the individuals in a unit; it also defines the area in which procedural and substantive agreements negotiated by an employer (or employers) and a union (or unions) will apply; and it also enables employees to know with whom they are grouped for negotiating purposes.

10. The CIR is aware that when it recommends a particular bargaining unit more extensive bargaining arrangements may already have been established or be desirable in the future. On the other hand, some groups of employees within a unit may have a particularly strong common interest which is not shared by other employees and so separate bargaining arrangements covering specific issues may need to be made for them within a bargaining unit. Whether a group of employees should constitute a "bargaining unit" rather than being covered by separate arrangements within a wider unit is a question which concerns the degree to which it has a distinct identity and interest from other groups. It also depends upon the willingness of an employer or a union or unions to have separate negotiating arrangements for different groups of employees which could eventually lead to the fragmentation of established negotiating machinery.

11. A careful and systematic assessment also needs to be undertaken before recommendations are made for the recognition of bargaining agents. This requires a detailed analysis of each case and in Chapter 3 we examine the Commission's approach to these issues. The Commission has been especially concerned to make recommendations which will further order and stability in industrial relations by ensuring that recommended agents have sufficient support in the units which they seek to represent, and that they are independent and effective organisations. Prospective bargaining agents have, therefore, had to meet three standards before recognition is recommended: they should have adequate support in the unit, they should be independent, and they should be effective. The CIR has assessed employee opinion in potential bargaining units to discover whether there is sufficient support for an agent and carried out detailed investigations into the organisation and structure of the unions or staff associations claiming recognition.

12. In practice bargaining unit and agency questions are not as distinct as this analysis might suggest because the presence of core groups provides a common link between them. No bargaining unit question arises where there is no support for collective bargaining or for a particular agent or agents. The core group concept is central to bargaining unit issues because each unit needs to be based on at least one core group which has sufficiently strong common interests to support effective collective bargaining. This concept may also be linked to the problems of the bargaining agent because one of the ways in which the common interests of a core group may be expressed is by means of membership and support for a trade union. Both an appropriate unit and an appropriate agent may be strongly suggested in a situation by trade union membership and the attitudes of employees to prospective bargaining agents. To the extent that this is so the handling of recognition cases can be seen as a single process. However many of the considerations which arise in the determination of the number of units and their precise boundaries require a detailed analysis which takes into account many factors in addition to trade union membership.

13. The CIR has gained wide experience of handling references in which issues of bargaining units and bargaining agents have played an important part. These issues have been of major importance in more than 60 pre- and post-Act cases most of which have been recognition references. However bargaining unit issues have also been important when the CIR has made recommendations for the reform of joint procedures in a company. This was because the CIR had to consider the level at which joint negotiating machinery should be established in a company and the employees who were to be covered by it. Decisions had to be made about whether or not to include particular groups in wider plant or company units; and whether there was a need to consolidate existing fractional bargaining arrangements into clearly defined units.

14. When the CIR was established as a Royal Commission in 1969 it was clear that it would be closely involved in disputes concerning trade union claims for recognition. This was so for a number of reasons. As the relative importance of plant level bargaining increased at the expense of national negotiations employees who had not previously had trade union representation at local level began to press for it. Non-wage issues such as work rules and discipline were becoming increasingly important in collective negotiations, and in order to pursue these issues at the workplace trade unions had to be recognised at this level. Also, as the Donovan Commission* had shown, that white-collar employees were joining trade unions in increasing numbers and were beginning to provide the main areas of trade union growth. This meant that white-collar claims for union recognition would become more frequent.

15. Although it had been public policy since the end of the First World War to encourage trade union organisation and collective bargaining no single body had been set up specifically to do this. Recognition disputes had either been handled confidentially by officials of the Ministry of Labour (later the Department of Employment) or by *ad hoc* courts or committees whose findings and recommendations were presented in official reports. When the Commission was set up, a body was created which was committed to the extension of trade union recognition wherever it was appropriate and which would publish reports on the references which it then received from the Secretary of State for Employment. From its inception until the Industrial Relations Act came into operation in November 1971, the Commission handled 13 references which were mainly concerned with recognition†. One of these references arose from a claim by the Association of Scientific, Technical and Managerial Staffs (ASTMS) to represent supervisors and method improvement officers in a firm in the petro-chemical industry. Four concerned recognition claims in small engineering companies while a further four references were in miscellaneous industries. Two references concerned claims by white-collar workers in insurance

---

*Royal Commission on Trade Unions and Employers' Associations 1965-68.
†See Appendix I.

companies and another the representation of scientists in a government research organisation. Finally, one reference concerned a nation-wide retail company with a large number of stores.

16. The references that the CIR handled during this early period gave it varied experience in a number of industries covering various kinds of employment and a number of interesting issues arose which had to be considered before recommendations could be made, e.g. Commercial Union, where questions concerning the independence of a staff association had to be examined. In another reference, Medical Research Council employees were members of a number of representative organisations and arrangements had to be devised to meet this situation. In these and other references recommendations had to be made which were appropriate for very different sets of circumstances.

17. It was during the period as a Royal Commission (1969-71) that the CIR developed its methods for handling recognition references which it continued to refine after the introduction of the Act. The methods used were related to the nature of the issues which arose. For instance, in many of the early references recognition claims had been made by a single union on behalf of relatively clearly-defined groups of employees at a single establishment. A requirement in these cases was to discover how much support the claimant union enjoyed among employees in terms of membership or potential membership. Techniques had to be developed for assessing employee support which were sufficiently flexible to meet the needs of different situations. It was also necessary to decide which employees should be grouped together for negotiating purposes and detailed factors relevant to this had to be examined. Criteria also had to be developed to assess the independence and effectiveness of potential agents. This meant that detailed inquiries had to be conducted before any recommendations could be made.

18. The introduction of the Industrial Relations Act did not lead to any changes in the techniques which had been developed for determining recognition references*. The terms "bargaining unit" and "bargaining agent"†, relatively new in the language of British industrial relations, were given wide currency by the Act but they referred to concepts which were already well established. However, the legislation and its balloting provisions increased the need for greater precision in formulating recommendations in recognition cases than had previously been required.

---

*See Appendix Ia.

†A "bargaining unit" was defined in the Act as: *those employees or descriptions of employees of an employer, or of two or more associated employers, in relation to whom collective bargaining in respect of such matters as are not dealt with under more extensive bargaining arrangements, is, or could appropriately be, carried on by an organisation of workers or a joint negotiating panel, or partly by a joint negotiating panel;* [Section 44(a)]. and a "sole bargaining agent": *in relation to a bargaining unit, means the organisation of workers or joint negotiating panel having negotiating rights in relation to that unit to the exclusion of all other organisations of workers and joint negotiating panels, except in respect of matters which are dealt with under more extensive bargaining arrangements.* [Section 44 (c)].

6

19. The approach that the CIR adopted in its handling of bargaining unit questions was to identify the factors giving rise to common interests among groups of employees and to consider their importance in particular cases. Although it is possible to identify specific factors, e.g. management organisation or a payments system, it is not practicable to treat them in isolation when future bargaining arrangements are under consideration. The importance of any single factor depends upon the circumstances of a particular case and its significance is derived from the importance attached to all the factors taken together. Moreover, the importance of particular factors depends upon the objectives being pursued by the parties. This means that a careful judgement has to be made of the views of the parties and of the relative importance they attach to different factors when bargaining unit recommendations are being formulated. If too much importance is wrongly given to one factor rather than another then a recommended bargaining unit may be unstable and eventually lead to the fragmentation of a proposed unit. An experienced independent agency can often assist the parties to arrive at an appropriate unit because it is able to assess the views of the parties and can also decide what other information is needed to help them to arrive at a reasonable arrangement. Chapter 2 provides a reference point for those faced with bargaining unit questions by examining the way in which these issues have been assessed by the CIR.

20. In agency questions there was little need to conduct detailed inquiries into the independence and effectiveness of TUC-affiliated unions since they had already established themselves as *bona fide* unions. The main issue for consideration in pre-Act references concerned the current membership of a union and potential membership levels among the employees it sought to represent. The question of support levels for a potential agent remained a key issue under Act references and surveys of employee opinion were an important feature of CIR inquiries.

21. Questions concerning the independence and effectiveness of a trade union or any other employee representative organisation are important when there is no public record of its history and negotiating experience and detailed inquiries then have to be undertaken. Although the Registrar of Trade Unions and Employers' Associations had to be sure that a union was financially independent before it was accepted on to the register, detailed inquiries into the operational independence or effectiveness of organisations claiming to represent employees were not undertaken. Since the CIR aimed to achieve a lasting settlement of recognition issues, it had to be sure that any organisation that was recommended as a bargaining agent would be able to effectively represent its members. If an organisation was not independent or effective it would be unable to adequately represent its members who might eventually seek the representation of another organisation and this could lead to unstable bargaining arrangements. In the Commercial Union reference the key question which had to be considered concerned the independence and thus the effectiveness of a domestic staff association. In the William Hill reference a question arose

about the adequacy of the financial resources of The Union of Book-makers' Employees (TUBE) and whether they were sufficient for the union to represent its members. At the time TUBE was a new union which was not yet fully established.* It was clear that these questions required close examination when an organisation was newly established, if it were a staff association confined to a single private sector employer and especially if it seemed to be competing for members with an already well-established union.

22. Chapter 3 examines the main issues that the CIR has considered when assessing arguments in favour of a bargaining agent: independence, effectiveness and employee support levels. It is not self-evident which factors are relevant to the consideration of these questions and the analysis brings out the factors and arguments that have been raised in references. The ways in which the CIR has assessed employee support levels are also examined.

23. A clear agreement between an employer and a trade union on union recognition, the shape and coverage of a bargaining unit, and on the agent that is to represent employees in the unit has a number of advantages for the parties and also for the public interest. The advantages arise from the stability that clear recognition agreements can introduce into a situation which might otherwise be confused and uncertain.

24. The main advantages to an employer are that:

(i) future conflict over recognition issues can be avoided by agreeing to recognise trade unions and to set up joint bargaining arrangements;

(ii) where agreements can be reached with an independent and effective union the emergence of competitive unionism can be avoided;

(iii) where the agent is a multi-union panel agreements on spheres of influence can be concluded by the unions;

(iv) the future development of multi-union situations can be avoided;

(v) conflicts of loyalty sometimes arise among management grades especially in a developing collective bargaining situation. If an employer makes clear that he accepts the principle of collective bargaining and trade union membership for these grades of employees potential conflicts of loyalty can be reduced;

(vi) industrial relations policy-making can be developed more coherently when it is clearly understood which employees are to be covered by which agreements and arrangements; and

(vii) the negotiation of agreements, their implementation and servicing can be carried out much more effectively where there are clearly-defined bargaining units and arrangements.

---

*After conducting a ballot of its members in July 1974, TUBE is now to amalgamate with and form a separate section of the Association of Clerical, Technical and Supervisory Staffs, the white-collar section of the Transport and General Workers Union.

25. Trade unions gain advantages from having clearly-defined agreements covering recognition and bargaining arrangements because:

(i) membership can be increased and maintained more easily once a recognition agreement has been concluded;

(ii) problems of competitive union recruitment can be avoided;

(iii) union full-time officials have less difficulty in servicing their members;

(iv) union facilities can be negotiated more easily when membership boundaries are clear; and

(v) clearly understood and stable long-term negotiating arrangements can be developed with an employer.

26. The Commission has already made known its views on the advantages of collective bargaining as a means of resolving industrial relations issues. In its annual reports, in reports on particular references and in a general study of white-collar recognition based on the engineering and chemicals industries the CIR has indicated some of the ways in which employers and trade unions can handle these questions. Taken together these reports provide valuable guidance on trade union recognition since they cover a variety of different circumstances.

27. The present study does not set out to review the detailed methods and techniques that have been used by the Commission in its conduct of recognition references. Neither does it seek to show how day-to-day issues that arose during the course of references were handled. The aim of the paper is less wide-ranging since it is confined to an examination of the factors which have received detailed consideration in the assessment of potential bargaining units and of the qualifications of bargaining agents to represent employees. Such an examination will be of interest to a number of groups who are concerned with the development and reform of procedures for the conduct of collective bargaining. Practitioners such as employers, employers' associations and trade unions will have a guide to the factors that require consideration before detailed bargaining arrangements are established. These practitioners and students of industrial relations will be able to see how a public body with a commitment to the orderly development of collective bargaining has taken account of various factors and arguments that arose during its handling of recognition references. They will also be able to see how the CIR interpreted its terms of reference and legislative provisions and the way in which public policy on trade union recognition has been developed. Finally, a study such as this can provide guidance to those in government who have to make future provision for the handling of union recognition claims by an independent third party body concerned with the orderly extension of collective bargaining.

2 The determination of bargaining units

(i) Factors in the determination of bargaining units

28. The Introduction to this study has shown that bargaining units are fundamental to orderly collective bargaining arrangements. Trade unions need to know whom they represent and on whose behalf they are negotiating. Employers need to know which groups of their employees are represented by particular unions or negotiating panels and what the coverage of collective agreements is intended to be. It is also important for groups of employees to know how they are represented and what agreements they are covered by. Where membership boundaries are unclear the potential exists for inter-union jurisdictional conflicts, competitive union recruitment and the breakdown of bargaining arrangements which can harm all interests. It is thus important to ensure that appropriate bargaining units are established early in the recognition process. Appropriate bargaining units can contribute to order and stability in industrial relations in a firm and considerable thought needs to be given by employers and trade unions to what may be "appropriate" in each case.

29. It has also been shown in the previous Chapter that there are no simple solutions to problems about which employees should be grouped together for bargaining purposes. The development of industrial relations in each company has to be taken into account as well as many other factors which influence the behaviour and views of employers, trade unions and their members. The purpose of the present Chapter is to analyse the factors which have influenced the Commission's decisions in the recognition cases it has handled. It should not however be forgotten that when making detailed enquiries the Commission has always been aware of the particular industrial relations situation that it has been examining. An important aspect of CIR inquiries is that it has paid attention to detail while retaining a broader view of the objectives being pursued by the parties in a case as well as the requirements of public policy.

30. In this section of the Chapter we consider the nature of the factors which are relevant to the determination of bargaining unit issues. We argue that individual factors cannot be taken in isolation and that a number of factors have to be assessed together to decide what unit or units are appropriate in any situation. The argument is also put forward that the importance of factors is derived from particular situations and also from the objectives being pursued by the parties and any third party involved in

conciliating recognition cases. The next section outlines the issues which the Commission has faced in considering what the potential bargaining units are and how far they should extend. We go on to consider the frequency with which various factors have arisen in Commission references. The remaining sections describe these factors in more detail and show how they have arisen in particular references.

31. Before considering the factors which are relevant in the determination of the shape of bargaining units it is necessary to indicate what these factors are. The Code of Industrial Relations Practice gives some guidance about the factors which might be taken into account in deciding which groups of employees should be associated together in units*. Generally speaking bargaining units should cover as wide a group of employees as practicable since too many small units make it difficult to ensure that related groups of employees are treated consistently†. However, the Code points out that although the interests of employees covered by a bargaining unit need not be identical there should be a substantial degree of common interest between them. Bargaining units should not be unnecessarily small but they should not be enlarged at the expense of including diverse groups with no interests in common‡.

32. The Code summarises a number of factors which should be taken into account when defining bargaining units§. These factors need to be considered if the boundaries of units are to be realistic in the light of employees' own ideas of their interests and are to relate to the organisational structures and policies of employers and trade unions. The following factors are listed in the Code: ‖

(i) the nature of the work;
(ii) the training, experience and professional or other qualifications of the employees concerned;
(iii) the extent to which they have interests in common;
(iv) the general wishes of the employees concerned;
(v) the organisation and location of the work;
(vi) hours, working arrangements and payment systems;
(vii) the matters to be bargained about;
(viii) the need to fit the bargaining unit into the pattern of union and management organisation;
(ix) the need to avoid disruption of any existing bargaining arrangements which are working well;
(x) whether separate bargaining arrangements are needed for particular categories of employees, such as supervisors or employees who represent management in negotiation.

---

*Industrial Relations: Code of Practice, paragraphs 74-81.
†Ibid, paragraph 76.
‡Op.cit, paragraph 77.
§Ibid paragraph 78.
‖Ibid paragraph 78.

33. In any situation a number of these factors will be influential in determining the shape of bargaining units which might be recommended. No single factor will be of such fundamental importance that it will by itself lead to a recommendation contrary to that suggested by other factors. Some factors, such as union membership or the presence of existing bargaining arrangements which are working well, may be of considerable importance in particular cases but even these will have a restricted influence for two main reasons. First there is a need to decide how many units are appropriate to a particular case. Second when there is a need to decide the precise extent of units even the most important factors in a situation may not provide answers to these questions. For example, union members in a company may be divided into two units if other factors suggest this is most appropriate. In another case it may be appropriate to exclude some employees who were covered by previously established arrangements from a newly established unit or to include others who were not covered by existing arrangements. These decisions depend on a complex of factors and what has to be looked for is the dominant set of factors in each case, not a single dominant factor.

34. One possible set of circumstances may be described as an example. A bargaining unit could be recommended for a group of employees doing similar work, on the same wage payment system and with other common terms and conditions. These factors are especially important in identifying work groups and may help to point to appropriate units. But the decisive factors may be that these employees constitute a distinct group in the management organisation and would prefer to be associated together. These last two factors would be most important in a decision for these employees to be grouped together but the other factors would also be important in support of the decision.

35. Although it is important to establish which set of factors is the most influential in a given situation another question remains: how is their importance to be recognised? There has to be a frame of reference for selecting the factors to be taken into account when deciding what the possible units are and which is likely to be the most appropriate unit if there is more than one possible unit.

36. A key question which arises in the determination of bargaining units concerns the relative importance of factors and two contrasting viewpoints can be identified. On the one hand factors may be given weightings of relative importance *a priori*. On the other hand the relative importance of factors can be derived entirely from the circumstances of a particular case. However both of these views are inadequate because in practice factors derive their relative importance from two main sources. The first is the particular situation in a company or undertaking under examination. The second are the long-term objectives being pursued by the parties in the determination of bargaining units. The significance of any factor arises from the outcome of these two sources.

37. The nature of the relationship between fact and purpose and its implications may be illustrated by an example. If one of the main purposes being pursued is the maintenance of existing bargaining arrangements where they are working well then great importance will be placed on the presence of such arrangements when they arise in situations under study. Consequently the scope of these arrangements is likely to be a relatively important factor in determining a unit.

38. A second example of the relationship between fact and purpose may be given using "acceptability to the parties" as a major goal in determining units. When this is an important objective the management organisation of a firm and the scope of trade union membership would become relatively more important factors than they might elsewhere since these factors are likely to reflect the parties own wishes.

39. The importance of the factors in these examples will vary according to (i) the facts of the case and (ii) the priority given by the parties to the suggested objectives.

40. Existing bargaining arrangements would not be an important factor in the first example where maintaining existing bargaining arrangements is an important objective if there were no such arrangements or if the existing arrangements were working badly and were clearly inadequate. In the second example, where acceptability to the parties is an important objective, the absence of clear divisions in the management structure renders this factor of little significance (except to support a company-wide unit). Similarly, low levels of union membership or a confused membership pattern would reduce the importance of the union membership factor if an attempt was being made to relate the unit to union membership.

41. The priority given to various objectives can have a big influence on the relative importance of factors—indeed it determines which factors are considered. This can be seen by referring again to the previous examples. In the first case the preservation of existing arrangements may become less important than, for example, consolidating bargaining arrangements. Such arrangements would not constitute an important factor if these arrangements tended to fragment a situation. Thus factors which influence the extent of a consolidated unit would be more significant in this kind of situation.

42. The effect of a change in priorities can also be illustrated if "acceptability to the parties" were not the dominant consideration in the second example. Taking the "maintenance of existing bargaining arrangements" as the main priority "management organisation" as a factor would become less important if the existing arrangements were out of line with this organisation. The facts of the case would however be the same.

43. The importance of factors then varies both with the facts of the case and with the priorities given to possible objectives. The facts in each case are unique so that no assertions can be made about the relative importance of factors *a priori*; but the assessment of which facts are important in a case will depend on the objectives which are being pursued by employers, unions and third parties.

44. The objectives which are to be pursued and their order of priority are policy matters which have to take account of the particular circumstances of a case. Possible objectives in the determination of bargaining units include the following:

(i) establishing units which are acceptable to the parties including the employees;

(ii) ensuring that union recognition will be achieved;

(iii) establishing units which will be viable in the long term;

(iv) ensuring that units accord with the management organisation of a company;

(v) ensuring that units accord with a trade union organisation structure;

(vi) maintaining existing bargaining arrangements where they are working well.

45. This list is not exhaustive of all the objectives that can be pursued in the determination of bargaining units. Nor does it imply that all of these objectives have to be pursued. Indeed the circumstances in particular cases will mean that some objectives may at times be unattainable. For example, a unit which is acceptable to employees and trade unions in a specific case may not necessarily be the one which most neatly fits management structure. What the Commission has had to do in resolving bargaining unit issues has been to pursue objectives which are attainable in the light of the industrial relations history in particular cases using the factors as a guide to what is appropriate.

46. Generally the Commission has been able to establish through its inquiries what are likely to be the most appropriate objectives in a case. Generally units in which there is majority support for recognition are those which are most likely to be viable in the long-run. This is because substantial levels of support for collective bargaining and of actual and potential trade union membership are the strongest indications which may be available that there is support for a union claiming recognition. At the same time these factors indicate that there is sufficient interest to support collective bargaining in the future. Such units are also likely to be acceptable to the claimant union though there will occasionally be employers opposed to the principle of recognition or the recognition of particular unions. The Commission has found that in most although not all cases it has been possible to formulate proposals which are acceptable to employers and to the union(s) recommended for recognition. The

remaining objectives such as maintaining existing bargaining arrangements which are working well have also been attainable where they have been of important practical significance.

(ii) Bargaining unit issues and the factors the CIR has used in determining them

47. In this section we relate the general analysis in the first part of the Chapter to the experience of the CIR. In particular we draw attention to the frequency with which factors have arisen in CIR recognition references. It has been argued that the importance of factors depends on the facts of each separate case and the objectives which are being pursued and that no generalisations can be made about the importance of factors *a priori*. However it is useful to know how often factors have arisen in various cases in the past since it suggests what factors may require attention in the future. Consequently CIR references have been examined to discover how frequently particular factors arose in the determination of bargaining unit questions. This analysis is presented in the latter part of this section.

48. Before considering the frequency with which factors have been relevant in the determination of bargaining unit problems, it is necessary to have a clear idea about the forms which these problems can take. This is important since the relevance of a factor and its influence in particular cases can only be assessed if there is a clear idea of the bargaining unit issues that can arise. The issues to be examined here are essentially questions about which groups of employees should be associated together for bargaining purposes as opposed, for example, to questions about what bargaining arrangements should be established or what the subject matter of negotiations should be.

49. Questions about which groups of employees should be associated together for bargaining purposes arise in a number of closely-related forms. When answering these questions it is necessary to decide whether there are any groups of workers in the situation who clearly ought to be covered by the same negotiating process if a bargaining unit were to be established. Such groups will have strong and apparent common interests and will often have demonstrated a desire for collective representation by joining trade unions, by a past history of negotiating with their employers, and possibly by participation in industrial action. These groups will frequently be easy to identify because their members perform similar tasks, possess a shared work experience, skills or qualifications, or work under common terms and conditions of employment. These factors might suggest that there should be a bargaining unit solely for the members of such a group. However this course of action could tend to encourage fractional bargaining, and employers, trade unions and third parties may prefer to see bargaining units extended beyond one distinct work group although this group will constitute the "core" of the unit.

50. Bargaining units may be extended beyond core groups in two ways. One is to include individuals and groups who would not be capable of supporting bargaining by themselves but share some common interests with the core group. For example, they might be paid under a common payment system or work in the same branch of an organisation as the members of a core group. Similar factors might also suggest that two or more core groups could be linked together to establish a wider unit. Groups may be linked in either of these ways provided that there is a minimum of shared common interests and that if necessary any distinct interests are taken into account by special arrangements within a unit.

51. If a core group cannot be extended either by including other employees who could not constitute core groups themselves or by linking it with other core groups it may not be possible to establish a bargaining unit. Although there may be a group of employees with strong common interests in an organisation, possibly a group of union members, other factors may suggest that this group by itself is inadequate for the purposes of forming a bargaining unit and supporting collective bargaining.

52. A number of examples of this situation were found by the CIR. Some of them arose because core groups defined by union membership and concentrated geographical location were impossible to distinguish for bargaining purposes because they were small in numbers in relation to the whole organisation, terms and conditions of employment were settled on a company-wide basis, or because the members of the core groups were in other ways closely related to other employees. Such cases included the Anglia Building Society and Norwich Union references.* A variation of this situation arises where union membership in an organisation suggests a core group may be present but on closer examination its membership is found to be scattered among the employees in such a way that they share no common interests which distinguish them as a group from other employees. If the level of union membership is low in relation to the total number of employees then it is possible that no group could be identified which could form the core of a bargaining unit. Such situations arose in the pre-Act case Electric Windings and in the Ken Hailes, Roland Jones and Temperance Permanent Building Society references.†

53. If a core group is not found to be an appropriate group by itself for bargaining purposes then three possibilities arise. These are that:

(i) no bargaining unit can be recommended;

(ii) the core group could be extended to include other groups in order to create a viable unit; or

(iii) two or more core groups may be associated together to constitute a viable unit.

---

*CIR Reports No. 79 and 82.
†CIR Reports No. 21, 72, 73 and 75.

The extension of core groups by either method (ii) or (iii) has provided the CIR with some of its main questions when it has had to consider bargaining unit issues.

54. When deciding how far a core group can be extended or whether two or more such groups may appropriately be associated together four possible forms of extension can be considered. The unit may be extended along organisational lines, i.e. across organisational boundaries within a company or linking employees in related companies in a group. Alternatively other groups of workers could be included who are either above or below the core groups in the hierarchy of the firm (a vertical extension of the unit); or whose status is equal to theirs (horizontal extension). Another possibility is that workers who have similar status and job content and work in the same division of an organisation, but work in different locations, may be incorporated (geographical extension).

55. Four questions have to be resolved when a core group or groups are being identified and considered for inclusion in a bargaining unit. These questions were not handled in a mechanistic way by the CIR but they have to be considered whenever recognition claims are examined. The four questions concern:

(i) the organisational extent of a potential bargaining unit;

(ii) the geographical extent of a potential bargaining unit;

(iii) the vertical extent of a potential bargaining unit;

(iv) the horizontal extent of a potential bargaining unit.

56. In any particular reference more than one issue may arise and these may be of different types. The most common combinations are organisational with geographical issues and vertical with horizontal issues. Typical of the first possibility are problems of how units should be extended across the organisational structure of a company which has geographically based divisions. An example of the second of these possibilities is an issue about whether a unit should be extended from manual production workers to include lower levels of supervision, as well as horizontally to include maintenance workers. Two issues of the same type may also be present. Whether, for example, a bargaining unit based on a core of clerical workers should be considered for extension to include supervisors or manual ancillary staff such as porters or cleaners. The CIR has reported on situations where many such issues and combinations of issues have had to be resolved.

57. Two examples of issues of organisational extent may be found in the Horizon Holidays reference.* In this case there was a strongly unionised group of employees at the Acton office of the company and

*CIR Report No. 43.

ASTMS were seeking to be recognised on behalf of this group. However, the Commission found that there were employees of two other companies which were part of the Horizon group* who were also at Acton and doing similar work. Some of these employees were also members of ASTMS. Taking these and other factors into consideration the Commission recommended a unit which included employees of all three companies and so extended across formal organisational boundaries.

58. The second issue of organisational extent which arose in the Horizon Holidays reference was whether to include employees of the companies who worked in other London offices and in the branch offices throughout the country. This was an organisational issue because the Acton offices were managed separately from the other offices. There was also a geographical aspect which is often the case where companies base their organisational structure at least partially on geographical considerations. Although a unit extending beyond Acton might have been appropriate the Commission decided not to recommend a unit for the whole company because support for collective bargaining was limited outside the Acton offices. Consequently the recommended unit did not extend across these particular geographical and organisational boundaries.

59. A number of other recognition references provide instances of issues arising about the organisational extent of units. Many of these issues, like those in Horizon Holidays, had geographical aspects. Some references where such issues were especially important included Allied Breweries; William Hill; Ken Munden; Seymour and Story; and the Anglia Building Society.†

60. Not all organisational issues had important geographical dimensions. The first of the two issues described above in Horizon Holidays, for example, did not. Another example was in the Barclays International reference, where the staff association raised the possibility of grouping employees in Barclays International with those of Barclays Bank Limited in one unit.‡ The Commission did not recommend that this should be done. Although there were links between them the two Barclays banks were organisationally distinct, operating independently and performing different functions, and there were separate histories of collective bargaining.

61. There were a number of instances of bargaining unit issues arising over the grouping of geographically-separated employees who were nevertheless part of a common organisational structure. One example of this

---

*These companies were Horizon Travel and 4S Travel. The original reference from the Industrial Court did not cover these companies but the scope of the reference was extended to include them.

†CIR Reports No. 38, 63, 64 and 79.

‡CIR Report No. 58. Although Barclays International mainly operated in London, many offices and branches of Barclays Bank are also, of course, situated there. Consequently there was no important geographical issue.

was found in the second of the Associated Octel references* where the issue was whether supervisors and method improvement officers employed at Northwich and Amlwch should be included in a bargaining unit consisting mainly of similar employees at Ellesmere Port. The Commission decided that they should be included in a single bargaining unit with those at Ellesmere Port.† This was acceptable to the parties and consistent with the similarity of their duties, salary structure, grading schemes and other conditions of employment.

62. Issues about the vertical extent of units have mainly arisen over questions about how far bargaining units should extend into supervisory and management groups. An early report, BSR Limited, drew attention to this problem suggesting that there may often be a need for separate arrangements. On many subsequent occasions the Commission has had to indicate the point at which a "line" should be drawn excluding managers from a unit comprised of employees they supervise. Some of the reports which include discussion about where this "line" should be drawn are C. A. Parsons, Coventry Economic Building Society, Connor and Forbes, Barclays International, and the Temperance Permanent Building Society‡.

63. The Medical Research Council (MRC) reference provides an example of another form that issues about the vertical extent of units can take.§ In this case the work groups involved included various levels of scientist, clinical and non-clinical, and technicians. The vertical hierarchy was based less on supervisory responsibilities, although these were present, than on professional qualifications and status. It was necessary to decide whether particular groups should be represented by specialist organisations with separate bargaining units or whether they should all be included in the one unit. The Commission recommended that bargaining should take place for all of these employees of the MRC mainly on the grounds that their common interests, derived from working together on projects, were stronger than the distinctive features of the various groups.

64. The Parsons case raised issues both of the "vertical" and the "horizontal" extents of bargaining units. One of the problems was to identify the work groups, which could form the core of a bargaining unit. The United Kingdom Association of Professional Engineers (UKAPE) argued that the professional engineers employed by the Parsons companies had a "community of interest" which bound them together and distinguished them from the other technical employees with whom they had traditionally been grouped. UKAPE therefore argued that professional engineers should have a separate bargaining unit. This argument raised both "vertical" and "horizontal" questions because a unit for professional

---

*CIR Report No. 68.
†CIR Report No. 68, paragraphs 15 and 16.
‡CIR Reports No. 32, 42, 44, 58 and 75.
§This was a pre-Act reference (CIR Report No. 12). Consequently the term "bargaining unit" was not in use although the issue was essentially a "bargaining unit" one.

engineers would extend from non-managerial into managerial grades (above the "line"); and it would also have to be shown that "professional" engineers could be separated for bargaining purposes from those who were engaged on similar work but were not professionally qualified. Many factors in the situation suggested that it would not be appropriate for such a unit to be recommended. It was not appropriate to join together employees both above and below the line nor was the claim that professional engineers had a sufficiently-distinct community of interest established.

65. Two other cases involving the identification of the appropriate work groups to form the cores of bargaining units arose from the claims of the Association of Licensed Aircraft Engineers (ALAE) to represent licensed aircraft engineers.* Again both "vertical" and "horizontal" issues were raised. The "vertical" issue was whether the boundaries of the potential unit should include aircraft engineers only or whether it should be extended "downwards" to include employees who had not yet qualified for licensing as aircraft engineers. In both cases the CIR recommended that both groups should be included. The horizontal issues centred around which work groups, not being aircraft engineers should be associated with the core groups of aircraft engineers in possible wider units. The Commission decided that non-aircraft mechanics and stock clerks should be associated with the aircraft engineers in the Pan American unit. However technical "back-up" staffs were excluded from the Airline Engineering unit. The main factors in all of these issues were job-content, training and work experience, and past collective bargaining practices. The last of these was specially relevant in the Pan American case.

66. These are only some of the issues which have been examined by the Commission during the course of determining bargaining units. Some of the most relevant factors have also been indicated, although others were also taken into account. In the remainder of this Chapter we analyse the factors which can be relevant in determining bargaining units and examine the way in which criteria based on them have been used by the Commission to resolve issues of the kind which have been described. 28 issues of the organisational geographical, horizontal and vertical extent of units arising in 21 Section 46 cases have been examined in this study.

67. Sixteen factors have been identified for analysis. This list, although based on the Code, is slightly extended because in some cases the factors as they appear in the Code can be more conveniently sub-divided. The factors, with the number of times each factor has been relevant in determining the recommended units are as follows:†
  (i) Job skills and content (20)
  (ii) Payment systems (19)

---

*Pan American World Airways and Airline Engineering, CIR Reports No. 55 and 66.
†The maximum number of times a factor could have been relevant is 28, the total number of issues analysed.

20

(iii) Other common conditions of employment (19)
(iv) Employee preferences of association (13)
(v) General employee wishes towards collective bargaining (11)
(vi) The maintenance of existing collective bargaining arrangements which are working well (9)
(vii) Membership or non-membership of unions or staff associations (9)
(viii) Transfer patterns between different jobs (8)
(ix) The presence of procedures unilaterally operated by management (7)
(x) The training and experience of employees (5)
(xi) Management structure (5)
(xii) Promotion patterns (5)
(xiii) Geographical location (4)
(xiv) Qualifications and professionalism (1)
(xv) Physical working conditions (1)
(xvi) Recruitment source (1)

This list refers only to the number of times a factor has been found to be relevant to determining the shape of a bargaining unit which was eventually recommended. This list does not imply anything about the relative importance of a factor in any given case. Although "job skills and content", "payment systems", "other common conditions of employment" and "employee preferences" and "general wishes" have often been both relevant and important other factors which appear infrequently have occasionally been important.

68. The Commission has also had to consider arguments for bargaining units or in favour of boundaries for bargaining units which the Commission concluded were in the circumstances unconvincing. The factors on which these arguments were based and the number of issues to which these arguments were directed were as follows:

(i) Membership or non-membership of unions or staff associations (7)
(ii) Job skills and content (6)
(iii) Other common conditions of employment (6)
(iv) Payment systems (5)
(v) Qualifications and professionalism (4)
(vi) Employee preferences of association (3)
(vii) General wishes of employees towards collective bargaining (3)
(viii) Management structure (3)
(ix) Geographical location (3)
(x) The training and experience of employees (2)
(xi) The presence of procedures unilaterally operated by management (1)
(xii) Transfer patterns between different jobs (1)

Although some factors were frequently used in support of arguments which were not accepted this does not mean that these factors were unimportant. It only means that these factors have more often been of insufficient importance in particular situations and in relation to other factors to support recommendations in favour of certain units or boundaries.

69.   The 16 factors which have helped determine bargaining units can be conveniently grouped under three headings: factors which relate to the characteristics of work groups; those derived from trade union membership and collective bargaining arrangements; and factors which need to be taken into account if bargaining units are to be as far as possible in line with managerial structure and policy. Individual factors may thus be grouped as follows:

(a) *Factors relating to the characteristics of the work group*

job skills and content; payment systems; other common conditions of employment; the training and experience of employees; qualifications and professionalism; and physical working conditions.

(b) *Factors introduced by the presence of trade union membership and collective bargaining arrangements*

employee preferences of association; general employee wishes towards collective bargaining; the maintenance of existing collective bargaining arrangements which are working well; and membership or non-membership of unions or staff associations.

(c) *Factors based on management organisation and areas of decision-taking*

the presence of procedures unilaterally operated by management; management structure; promotion patterns; geographical location; and recruitment source.

70.   The first group of factors tends to form the basis of the work group organisation which may arise independently of management organisation. It has therefore been natural to consider these factors in deciding what bargaining units should be established. The introduction of trade unions and collective representation into a firm modifies situations and has to be taken into account. Finally managerial policy and institutions help to structure situations and provide sets of constraints for the future. Thus bargaining units have to be appropriate for the work groups, collective bargaining arrangements and the needs of efficient management.

71.   In the next three sections we examine these groups of factors. In each case the factors influencing positive bargaining unit recommendations are considered first. Then some of the factors which arose in arguments which were not accepted are examined. These sections are followed by a section in which we briefly outline the objectives of employers and trade unions in individual references and some of the arguments which they put forward in support of their own bargaining unit preferences.

(iii) The characteristics of the work group

72. Informal work group organisation is based on many factors which serve to give a group its identity; to reinforce the cohesion of its members; and to guide the development of the members' attitudes towards fellow employees, the employer and trade unions. It is necessary to take these factors into account when determining bargaining units if the units are to be in line with employees' perceptions about the way in which they are informally organised and with their wishes about how they should be grouped for representational purposes. Furthermore these factors—especially payments systems, physical working conditions and conditions of employment—generally constitute an important part of the subject matter of collective bargaining. If bargaining units and the arrangements which may be associated with them are to be appropriate to the subject matter of collective bargaining it is important that these factors should be examined when determining units.

73. The Commission has therefore considered the characteristics of the work group both to avoid recommending bargaining units which cut across employee workplace organisation and because these characteristics are related to the subject-matter of collective bargaining. In this section each of the six factors which are especially related to workplace organisation are individually examined but two points need to be kept in mind. First the factors have to be seen together to gain an adequate picture of workplace organisation in any situation and second the factors examined later in this Chapter concerning collective organisation and the organisation of the firm also influence the formation of work groups and the way they behave.

Job skills and content

74. "Job skills and content" arose in 20 of the 28 issues examined. In six of these issues arguments were also put forward based on job skills and content which were not accepted in the particular cases. In one issue (the organisational extent in Allied Breweries) the similarity of job skills and content was overruled by other factors and three units were recommended. This criterion has tended to be used for two major purposes. First to identify work groups to be considered for inclusion in bargaining units and second as a guide to the extension of bargaining units after core units have been identified. Only occasionally have job skills and content been decisive in delineating the unit itself.

75. In some cases the CIR considered that there should be a basic common work content linking the groups to be included in a bargaining unit. Common work content has not however been interpreted too rigorously. It has generally been considered sufficient that there should be some common techniques, responsibilities or skills; that the groups should be connected with the production of the same or similar types of products or provision of the same or similar types of services; or that they should work in reasonably close proximity.

76. This interpretation of the criterion may be traced to the first Associated Octel report when the Commission stated that "negotiating units"* should not reflect simple job demarcations. This approach was also reflected in the MRC report, where medically-qualified, scientific and technical staff were grouped together in a unit, the common job content consisting in the fact that they "worked closely together".†

77. The Section 46 references provide a variety of examples of the common job skills and content criterion. In Allied Breweries the common job content consisted in the responsibility for managing a public house. In Barclays International the employees were distinguished from Barclays Bank employees by the distinctive characteristics of overseas banking services. The broadly-similar functions of technicians provided a basis of common interest in the bargaining unit "below the line" in Parsons. A unit was determined in the Pan American reference on the grounds that employees all exercised some form of mechanics' skills.

78. Bargaining units have been extended beyond a core group on a number of variations of the job skills and content criterion. Relief managers were included in the bargaining units in Allied Breweries because, when they were working, their duties were exactly the same as those of the main body of managers. The stock clerks employed by Pan American at Heathrow were incorporated in the mechanics' unit partly on the grounds that they had to acquire some of the mechanics' knowledge in the course of their job. The company wide unit in Associated Octel was justified in part because the supervisors and method improvement officers at Amlwch and Northwich exercised the same responsibilities as their colleagues at Ellesmere Port. Numerous other examples of the use of this criterion may be found in the published reports.

79. Job skills and content have been decisive in determining the coverage of bargaining units on only a few occasions and have usually been used to exclude groups of managers or supervisors from units which included people they managed. Examples include Parsons, William Hill and other references where senior managers and supervisors were often excluded by mutual agreement. In one case, Bridgwater Building Society, this argument helped to justify a separate bargaining unit for branch managers. A variant of the argument occurred when head office supervisors employed by Coventry Economic were included in a unit with the people they supervised since they had limited managerial responsibilities.

80. One other case may be cited where job content was important in determining the shape of a unit. This was Con Mech, where the heavy manual nature of the work of the earth-moving equipment workers and some stores workers led to these groups being distinguished as a unit from office employees and employees engaged on bread-slicer production.‡

---

*CIR Report No. 1, paragraph 26.
†CIR Report No. 12, paragraph 74.
‡CIR Report No. 53.

24

81. Those cases where the job skills and content criterion was not considered important present a diverse picture. Two examples are found in Allied Breweries. The catering house managers were included in the units despite the company's argument that their skills were different from those of public house managers; and three bargaining units were recommended although the job content was common. In Coventry Economic a group of ancillary employees were included in the bargaining unit despite the different nature of their jobs (the main employee groups were clerical and administrative). In Pan American the technical and statutory duties of the licensed aircraft engineers were unsuccessfully put forward by the ALAE as reasons for a separate unit. In Barclays International the argument that the differing job skills of the computer, technical and non-clerical groups justified separate units for these groups was not accepted. In each of these examples arguments based on job-content were not accepted because combinations of other factors pointed towards different recommendations.

82. The job skills and content criterion therefore helps to identify work groups and to link them together in units. In only a few instances have arguments based on this criterion been considered of sufficient importance to decisively affect the shape of a unit. More often these arguments have been considered relatively unimportant.

Payments systems

83. The payment system was a relevant factor in 19 of the issues examined. In five issues arguments based on the payment system were put forward but not considered relevant.

84. The payments system factor has taken three main forms. First a payment system has normally been a relatively straight-forward determinant of a unit when the unit can be drawn to coincide with the boundaries of separate decision-taking processes regarding pay systems and levels. Allied Breweries provides one example of this, where the boundaries of the three company-wide units within the wider organisation corresponded to the three separate decision-taking processes regarding pay.* Another example is Horizon Holidays, where a separate procedure existed for approving pay at Acton.† The separate pay policies of Barclays Bank and Barclays International also helped to determine the outer organisational boundaries of the recommended unit.‡ In these cases distinct payment systems have been influential in the determination of the extent of units.

---

*CIR Report No. 38, paragraphs 51-64.
†CIR Report No. 43, paragraph 76.
‡CIR Report No. 58, paragraph 63.

5. A second form of the payments system criterion arises where a group of employees have their pay determined by a procedure which is distinct from the pay determination procedure for other groups within the organisation even though the point of managerial decision-making is common. Examples include the horizontal and vertical extent of units in the Pan American, Bridgwater Building Society, Parsons and Associated Octel references. The recommended units in these cases were all influenced to some extent by the fact that the pay of the groups concerned was or had been traditionally decided separately from that of other groups within these organisations.

86. Finally some groups were established as distinct bargaining units partly because they constituted distinguishable pay grades or classes although their wages were not determined by any formally-separate process from the wages of excluded groups. This consideration was relevant to issues of vertical and horizontal extent arising in the Coventry Economic, Con Mech, John Joyce and William Hill references.

87. Of these three categories into which the payment system factor may be sub-divided, the first type has played a major role in determining bargaining units. The second and third categories have been significant only to the extent that pay considerations have supported other criteria which have pointed towards similar recommendations.

Other common conditions of employment

88. The fact that terms and conditions of employment other than pay were shared among one or more groups of employees was considered a relevant factor in 19 of the issues examined. In six of these counter-arguments based on other conditions of employment grounds were not considered sufficiently important when taken into account with other factors.

89. In many cases the factor was covered by the statement that a group or groups shared common terms and conditions of employment or did not do so. Often this would be linked with the pay system, as in the satement that "pay and other conditions of employment are determined for the company as a whole". In general these conditions included pensions, sick pay schemes, hours of work, holiday pay, redundancy provisions, etc.

90. Much of what was said about pay as a criterion also applies to other conditions of employment. The factor has tended to perform the same function as the pay criterion. The locus and extent of decision-making for conditions have a similar significance (paragraphs 83 to 87) but other conditions have been less important in most reports than payments systems.

91.   There are several examples of the use of the common conditions argument worth noting. There is one case where conditions of employment pointed in a different direction from an argument based on the pay system factor. This occurred in Coventry Economic where branch managers and head office supervisors were included in a broader unit. Their salary levels (though not their pay system) differed from other employees but they had other substantive interests in common with the other employees. A second case of interest is William Hill where employees in the recommended unit had company-wide conditions of employment in common but there was not yet a common pay system. Finally common conditions of employment (like the common salary structure) was a significant factor in the decision to recommend a company-wide unit in Associated Octel.

The training and experience of employees

92.   There were five issues examined in which the fact that employees did or did not have some training or work experience in common was relevant to the determination of bargaining units.

93.   Four examples (two in each case) were found in Pan American and Airline Engineering. In these cases one of the reasons why the licensed engineers could not be distinguished from the unlicensed was that all had to undertake the same initial training. Work experience was also relevant to deciding which groups should or should not be members of the same bargaining units as the aircraft engineers. In the Pan American case it was found that much of the training and work experience of other mechanics was similar to that of the aircraft mechanics which suggested that all should be members of the same unit. In contrast the technical back-up staff employed by Airline Engineering did not share a common training or work experience with this firm's aircraft engineers and, had a unit been recommended, they would not have been included in it.

94.   A further example of this factor having an important influence was found in the Associated Octel reference. One of the arguments in favour of a company-wide unit for the supervisors and method improvement officers was that the employees at Northwich and Amlwch, like those at Ellesmere Port, had broadly similar shop-floor experience.

Qualifications and professionalism

95.   The only occasion on which qualifications and professionalism as a factor contributed to the determination of a bargaining unit occurred in Associated Octel. The question of whether the recommended unit should be extended to cover the supervisors and method improvement officers in the whole company was partly determined on the grounds that these groups on different sites had some qualifications in common.

27

96.   Arguments based on qualifications and professionalism have not been accepted to justify particular units on four occasions. The National Association of Licensed House Managers (NALHM) claim that the public house managers employed in all three Allied Breweries operating companies had a common "professionalism" was not considered strong enough to justify a single organisation-wide unit.* Many factors contributed to the decision that professional engineering qualifications did not by themselves justify a unit for professional engineers in Parsons.† Among these factors was the impossibility of defining a distinct group of jobs which distinguished professional engineers from other technical staff; the presence of common interests linking all technical staff; and the general practice in the engineering industry. A similar complex of factors told against the establishment of separate units for licensed aircraft engineers in the Pan American and Airline Engineering references.

97.   The qualifications factor may support conclusions reached on the basis of other factors and arguments but it has not been a sufficiently important factor to override contrary considerations based on a variety of other criteria.

Physical working conditions

98.   These have been relevant on only one occasion; to help distinguish those involved in heavy manual work at Con Mech from other employees who were less interested in collective representation.‡

(iv) The presence of trade union membership and collective bargaining arrangements

99.   Work groups exist in the absence of trade union organisation but when it is introduced in a firm it can have a considerable effect on the existing work group structure and the relations between these groups and management. For instance, work groups which previously had few common interests may become united by common trade union membership. Similarly when employees are organised by a trade union they develop common attitudes towards collective bargaining which help to distinguish those employees who might appropriately be included in bargaining units from others who might be excluded. A past history of collective bargaining carried out on behalf of some employees will also help to distinguish them from other employees. Factors derived from the presence and growth of trade union membership and from any previous collective representation are therefore important guides to the way in which employees perceive their interests and to what their wishes regarding bargaining units might be.

---

*CIR Report No. 38, paragraph 66.
†CIR Report No. 32, paragraph 56.
‡CIR Report No. 53, paragraphs 15 and 17.

100. In many cases the CIR assessed employee-attitudes towards the shape of bargaining units by asking employees about their preferences of association with different groups for bargaining purposes. Those employees who have joined trade unions can be expected to have formed opinions about the groups with whom they share common interests and so employee wishes have been an important factor leading towards CIR recommendations.

General employee wishes towards collective bargaining

101. The Code of Practice suggests that employee wishes should be taken into account and that their attitude towards bargaining is an important factor in determining units. General support for collective representation suggests that employees in a unit will be interested in the bargaining which is carried out on their behalf, and that a unit would be viable in the long term. Where large groups of employees are indifferent to collective bargaining, as in the Norwich Union reference, other factors have had to be considered before recommendations have been made.

102. General employee wishes towards collective bargaining has been used as a factor in determining units in 11 issues examined. It has been important in identifying the nature of the core group and in questions of extending the core to incorporate other groups. Otherwise its effect has been largely negative; where no support for bargaining exists there can be no unit or extension of a unit.

103. Among some groups, such as the bread slicer-blade producers in Con Mech, the cleaners in the Bridgwater Building Society and the provincial employees of Horizon Holidays, there was a clear lack of support for collective representation.* Majority opposition to collective bargaining was expressed by the head office managers in Coventry Economic (56 per cent. against and 37 per cent. for).† The attitudes of employees in these groups was an important factor leading to their exclusion from the recommended bargaining units.

104. In other cases the attitudes of members of work groups or grades of employees towards collective bargaining have been unclear. In two cases groups of employees who were on balance against collective bargaining for themselves were left outside a recommended bargaining unit. These were the assistant managers and managers above the line in Parsons and the managers in Horizon Holidays.

105. Several groups of employees whose attitudes to collective bargaining were unclear have been included in wider bargaining units. Some examples are found in the William Hill reference. Groups of area supervisors,

---

*Only 5 of the 20 cleaners in the Bridgwater case accepted the invitation to express their views. CIR Report No. 57, paragraph 16.

†CIR Report No. 42, paragraph 79.

senior managers, genie operators and clerical and administrative workers contained only minority support for collective bargaining but all were incorporated in a bargaining unit for William Hill employees.*

106. Clearly, majority support for collective bargaining has not been seen as an essential pre-requisite for incorporation in a bargaining unit. Other factors pointed strongly to the conclusion that these groups in William Hill should be included in the unit. Equally, other factors suggested that the management groups in Parsons and Horizon Holidays should not at that time be incorporated in any unit. The attitudes of any work group to bargaining, especially if they are not clear, must always be taken in the context of other factors in the total situation.

107. It should be noted that in the unit which was finally recommended in William Hill there was majority support for collective bargaining. The groups which were not in favour of collective bargaining constituted relatively small parts of the wider unit.†

108. As a criterion, employee support for collective bargaining has two clear roles beyond the identification of core groups. First it is important in excluding groups where there is substantial opposition to collective bargaining. Second majority support is an important indicator of the future viability of a unit determined largely by other factors. Where support for collective bargaining is not decisive, then other factors have been used to decide whether the group or groups concerned should be incorporated in any bargaining unit.

Employees preferences of association

109. The preferences of employees about which groups of employees they should be associated with for bargaining purposes were relevant to the determination of units in 13 cases. In three cases arguments based on this factor were not considered to be important when other factors were also taken into account.

110. It might be argued that employee preference should be the single most important factor in determining the shape of a unit. This argument has however a major flaw since employees have to be presented with a choice of possible units to enable their preferences to be assessed and these suggested units have to be based on other factors. Employee preference then is useful if there is a choice of possible units each of which is potentially viable on the basis of other criteria.

---

*CIR Report No. 63, Appendix 2, Table 3.
†CIR Report No. 63, paragraph 44.

111. A number of published reports contain examples of work groups being incorporated into wider units on the grounds that they did not wish to have their own separate units. These include public house managers above the "cut-off" line in Allied Breweries and the head office staff in John Joyce. Associated Octel and Pan American both provide examples of employee preferences for associations in wider groups helping to determine the shape of the unit. The majority of method improvement officers and supervisors in Associated Octel stated that they wished to negotiate together. In Pan American two distinct expressions of preference helped to decide that the unit should cover all mechanics and stock clerks. First only a minority of the licensed aircraft engineers were in favour of a unit for themselves alone. Second all of the groups other than aircraft engineers were in favour of an all-embracing unit.*

112. Two references contain examples of groups of employees who had separate units considered for them partly on the grounds of their own preferences. One group was the branch managers in Bridgwater Building Society who were recommended to have their own unit.† If a unit for the Board-appointed staff of Barclays International had been recommended, it might also have been a separate one.‡ It should be noted however that other factors supported these recommendations.

113. Two examples of unsuccessful arguments based on "employee preference" to justify particular units in the face of other factors can be found in Parsons and Pan American. UKAPE in the Parsons case claimed that "professional engineers" above and below the line would prefer to be associated together for collective bargaining purposes. The possibility of this unit, and hence the validity of this claim, was rejected on a variety of grounds, of which the most important was that "professional engineers" did not constitute definable work groups either above or below the line.§ The second example of an argument in favour of a unit based on these grounds being rejected arose out of the claim of the ALAE to represent licensed aircraft engineers. The wishes of aircraft engineers (licensed and unlicensed) were not accepted as important in the Pan American report.‖ In this case 54 per cent. of all aircraft and radio mechanics would have preferred their own unit but the CIR did not accept that this group possessed a sufficiently distinct identity, given the background of the employees, their experience and the history of collective bargaining.

114. Employee preferences have therefore been relevant only where there are distinct work groups which have to be identified by examining a number of factors. Where there are such groups employee preferences can be important in deciding whether the groups should constitute

---

*For the views of licensed and unlicensed aircraft engineers taken together see paragraph 113.
†CIR Report No. 57, paragraphs 32 to 34.
‡CIR Report No. 58, paragraph 75.
§CIR Report No. 32, paragraph 56.
‖CIR Report No. 66, paragraph 59.

bargaining units or whether they should be included in wider units. Where no identifiable work group exists but merely a number of employees delineated by, perhaps, a single factor, expressed preferences have not been decisive in bargaining unit recommendations.

The maintenance of existing collective bargaining arrangements which are working well

115. The maintenance of existing collective bargaining arrangements was relevant as a factor in the determination of nine issues which arose in five references. The bargaining arrangements included not only those in operation during the course of the reference but also those which had been established although no longer fully operational provided that these arrangements still influenced the terms and conditions of employment in the unit. In all cases the existence or prior existence of bargaining arrangements had a positive influence on the shape of the recommended bargaining unit.

116. In three references the issues were mainly determined because effective collective bargaining arrangements were already in existence. The recommendation that there should be a separate unit for the public house managers employed by the Ansell's division of Allied Breweries owed a lot to the three-year history of negotiations between Ansells and the Transport and General Workers Union (TGWU). The fact that managers above the "cut-off" line had also been covered by the agreements was also a factor leading to their inclusion in the unit. The same consideration applied to relief managers but although catering house managers had not previously been covered by these arrangements it was not a bar to their inclusion in the unit.

117. A history of separate collective bargaining in Barclays International helped to decide that it would not be included within a wider Barclays unit. Furthermore there was a single joint negotiating committee for Barclays International which suggested that the recommended unit should include most of the employees.

118. A history of independent bargaining by the branch managers in Bridgwater Building Society also led to a recommendation for a separate bargaining unit covering this group.

119. Previous collective bargaining arrangements which covered Pan American's Heathrow stock clerks and mechanics was relevant to the decision to recommend a unit covering all of these employees rather than a number of units for smaller groups.* This was despite the fact that the body which had negotiated on behalf of the mechanics and clerks had disbanded although when the report was published agreements negotiated under these arrangements were still in force.

---

*CIR Report No. 55, paragraph 85.

120. Finally the collective bargaining arrangements which were taken into account in the Parsons case differed in being industry-wide.* The recommendation of a bargaining unit for technical staff below the line accorded with practice in the engineering industry, including the procedural agreements to which the Amalgamated Union of Engineering Workers (Technical and Supervisory Section) (TASS) was a party.

121. Wherever it has been present as a factor, well-established bargaining arrangements have been important in determining the shape of recommended bargaining units.

Membership or non-membership of trade uions and staff associations

122. Both actual and potential trade union and staff association membership† has been taken into account in determining the shape of bargaining units. Nine bargaining unit issues have been determined at least partly on such grounds but arguments based on considerations of trade union membership have been relatively unimportant on seven other occasions.

123. The use of trade union membership as a criterion to determine bargaining units must be distinguished from using it to determine questions of bargaining agency. A different purpose is being fulfilled although the same facts are being referred to. As a determinant of bargaining units trade union membership may be a guide to common interests felt by employees and so is one of the factors to be taken into account in identifying work groups, establishing core groups and extending core groups. This is a distinct process from evaluating the support for possible agents once a unit has been decided.

124. The union membership criterion can be examined in the context of single and multi-union situations. In three cases, Horizon Holidays, Con Mech, and Davenport the location of actual trade union membership determined the core units. Limited actual and potential union membership was an important factor in the decision not to recommend the extension of core units to include employees beyond those at Acton in Horizon Holidays or over the whole of the Con Mech and Davenport sites. In the Gordon Nunns reference high actual and potential union membership identified a core unit which included all employees of the company.

125. Trade union membership in the John Joyce reference presents a similar picture to attitudes to collective bargaining as a determinant of the unit. Both actual membership and potential support for the union (TUBE) if it were recognised helped to identify the core unit of betting shop employees. However doubts could have arisen over the question whether the head office staff should be included since 10 of these 11

---

*CIR Report No. 32, paragraph 32.

†The term "trade union membership" in this section should also be taken to refer to staff association membership.

employees were not members of the union. Five said they would join the union if it were recognised, one would not, and five did not know what they would do.* Other factors overruled the suggestion that head office staff should be excluded from the unit on these grounds alone.

126. In the William Hill reference other factors contributed to the decision to include small groups in the bargaining units despite their lack of support for the union, TUBE. Attitudes to trade union membership were important in identifying the core unit although the main factor concerned potential rather than actual union membership. There were several small work groups employed in William Hill where only minorities said they would join the union if it were recognised.

127. In cases where minority groups of employees showed lack of support for the union involved, employees in the proposed unit as a whole showed a clear majority of union members or potential union members.

128. Although a number of references concerned multi-union situations, in only one of these has an argument based on considerations of trade union membership been used in determining a bargaining unit issue. In Parsons the fragmented and limited nature of union membership among employees above the line was a major objection to establishing a bargaining unit for these employees. The decision not to recommend a bargaining unit was re-inforced by the absence of any possibility of co-operation between the UKAPE alliance and ASTMS.†

129. In some references, although not specifically cited as a factor, union membership was a major consideration in identifying the core and determining the extent of units. For example, the branch managers of Bridgwater Building Society had their own staff association which had taken part in collective bargaining separately from other employees. This was an important factor in the recommendation that the managers should have their own unit.‡ There are points of similarity between this case and Allied Breweries. Separate collective bargaining for the public house managers employed by Ansells was partly based on the presence of TGWU members and the existing collective bargaining arrangements provided support for the recommendation that Ansells should constitute a separate bargaining unit.§ This recommendation was reinforced by the geographical concentration of TGWU membership and the degree of autonomy allowed to Ansells as a "management company".

130. Another point which arose is that although there was strong support for one union across the company separate units were recommended for the three "management companies". Although NALHM represented

---

*CIR Report No. 71, paragraph 23.
†CIR Report No. 32, paragraphs 74 and 75.
‡But NUBE was the recommended agent for this unit.
§See paragraph 116.

employees in the Ind Coope, Ansells and Tetleys divisions separate units were finally recommended because of the concentration of TGWU members, the autonomy of the three companies and geographical factors.

131. Trade union membership was not explicity included as a factor determining the eventual bargaining unit for the Pan American mechanics but the pattern of union membership in this case was nevertheless important. Membership of ALAE was restricted to the licensed engineers among whom it had a majority in membership. However some of these were also members of the AUEW and almost one-third were members of the AUEW only. There were therefore union membership links between the licensed mechanics and the wider group of mechanics. These considerations led to the decision to recommend an all-inclusive unit.

132. The presence of trade union support in terms of actual or potential members is important in identifying the core of a possible bargaining unit. Trade union membership can also be a factor in extending a unit to include other work groups although other factors will be relevant to this decision. But where trade union membership is limited and fragmented between mutually hostile unions it may not be possible to identify a core unit.

(v) Management organisation and areas of decision-taking

133. Factors based on the management organisation of a company and on the subject matter of bargaining are of particular concern in the determination of units for two main reasons. First these factors, like the characteristics of the work group and the influence of collective representation, affect the way in which work groups express their interests. Employees are influenced by their position in the organisation's structure, by their work location and by the personnel policies followed by the company. These factors contribute to employees' perceptions of their common interests and need to be taken into account in determining bargaining units.

134. The second reason why these factors are important in the determination of bargaining units is that the efficiency of the firm cannot be forgotten in the process of determining bargaining units. For instance, if bargaining units are drawn across established organisational lines, a company may have difficulty in reconciling the outcome of subsequent negotiations with managerial decision-taking within the organisation. Consequently a single unit for an organisation containing a number of autonomous operating sections might be inappropriate, as the Commission decided in Allied Breweries. Equally a company with central management control may prefer as few units as possible to avoid fragmentation. This last point has not featured prominently in published reports because there seems to have been a preference for establishing wide units unless there are important factors pointing to smaller units.

The presence of procedures unilaterally operated by management

135. Management operated procedures as a factor refers to cases where management's employment policy can be used as a guide in delineating work groups and determining which groups should be included in bargaining units. This was relevant to the issues raised in eight separate references and in all cases but one the eventual unit accorded with management policy.*

136. In some cases the management policy was well established in the form of clear-cut procedures or institutions. For instance a brewer/ manager consultative committee was established in each of the three companies within the Allied Breweries organisation. The Commission decided that these could provide the basis for company-wide bargaining if there were units for each company rather than one organisation-wide unit. The Acton office of Horizon Holidays was in many respects a separately-managed office where merit awards, grievance, disciplinary and other personnel matters were largely settled internally. Acton could consequently be distinguished from the other London and Provincial offices, although it was a part of the wider group of companies. On the other hand, the fact that William Hill operated group-wide grievance and disciplinary procedures and other personnel policies influenced the recommendation that there should be a group-wide unit rather than a number of company-wide units.

137. The management procedure criterion took a less explicit form in Associated Octel. A horizontal link between the supervisors and the method improvement officers was established partly because the company had "historically" always treated the MIOs as part of the supervisory group,† and representatives of the MIOs were also included in the Supervisory Forum.

138. The policies and procedures operated by management are likely to be especially important where a bargaining unit can be based on a sub-ordinate management unit within an organisation or could cover the whole organisation.

Transfer patterns

139. There were eight cases where bargaining units have been shaped in part to include groups of employees linked by a degree of transferability between jobs. In Pan American one of the major links between the various groups of mechanics was that they could apply to transfer from one work group to another. There were therefore examples of mechanics transferring between being an aircraft and a general mechanic which suggested that these groups should be included in one unit.

---

*The exception was Airline Engineering where management regarded the back-up staff as part of a group including airline mechanics. This group was not included in the unit that would have been recommended.

†CIR Report No. 68, paragraph 15.

140. In one case, Horizon Holidays, the absence of transfers between the London offices and the provinces emphasised the degree of geographical separation between the provincial employees and the employees in the recommended unit.* This was one of the factors that suggested that provincial employees should be excluded from the unit.

141. An example of an argument based on the transfer of employees which was not accepted in the determination of a bargaining unit was in Barclays International. The Barclays Bank Staff Association (BBSA) wanted a group-wide bargaining unit and in support of this it contended that employees were regularly transferred between Barclays Bank and Barclays International. This argument was not accepted because these transfers would become rarer as specialisation between the work of the two organisations increased and no evidence was produced of any transfers having taken place recently.

142. The transfer of employees between work groups may provide evidence that these groups should be linked in a bargaining unit but the strength of the evidence will depend on the regularity of the transfers and whether it is a two-way process.

Geographical location

143. Geographical location influenced the shape of recommended bargaining units in four cases and there were three occasions where geographical location was discounted as a significant factor.

144. The scatter of employees in small groups in diverse work places suggested that the travel office employees of Horizon Holidays and the Bridgwater Building Society cleaners should not be included in the recommended units. Conversely, in the Munden reference the concentration of union membership in the London area supported the recommendation that there should be a unit for these employees which would not include Sherman's employees in Wales.† The concentration of Gordon Nunn's employees in the Leeds branch of TUBE also suggested that they might constitute a viable unit. An argument which did not gain acceptance was a statement by Horizon Holidays that the London offices, including Acton, were to be unified on one site. This would have pointed to a London-wide unit. There was however no immediate prospect of this unification taking place. In Coventry Economic Building Society where many factors pointed to the establishment of a single bargaining unit there was not thought to be a case for separating groups on the basis of their separate location.‡

---

*CIR Report No. 43, paragraph 66.
†See paragraph 157.
‡CIR Report No. 42, paragraph 61.

145. Geographical location has not been a decisive factor in most cases examined by the CIR although it has arisen on a number of occasions. This does not mean, however, that geographical factors could not be important elsewhere.

Management structure

146. The managerial structure within an organisation over-and-above industrial relations arrangements has been influential on five occasions and arose for consideration on three others although failing to gain acceptance.

147. In the three references where an organisation was divided into largely autonomous companies the recommended bargaining units took account of this fact. The three units recommended for Allied Breweries were based on the three operating management companies within the organisation. Similarly, Barclays International possessed a high degree of autonomy from Barclays Bank. This autonomy provided a strong argument for restricting the recommended unit to Barclays International and for rejecting any unit linking the two companies. The provincial branches of Horizon Holidays were organised separately from the London offices and performed different functions, a fact which contributed to the decision to exclude these employees from any London-based unit.*

148. Horizon Holidays also provides an example where employees of three separate companies within a wider organisation were included in the same unit because employees worked on the same site, did substantially the same work, and terms and conditions of employment were being brought in line between the companies.† Other factors also suggested that the separation between the companies was nominal both from the point of view of the employees, and increasingly as far as day-to-day management was concerned.

149. Provided there is sufficient independence between the parts of an organisation there may be a strong case for separate units. Management structure can influence the shape of units quite fundamentally especially when the organisation is divided for geographical reasons.

Promotion patterns

150. Promotion patterns influenced bargaining unit recommendations in five issues. For example, part of the case for linking the supervisors and method improvement officers of Associated Octel was because both groups were promoted from the shop-floor. Similarly if a unit had been recommended for the employees of Airline Engineering it would have included both licensed and unlicensed engineers partly because all members of this group were subject to the same promotion policy, and being unlicensed

---

*CIR Report No. 43, paragraph 67.
†CIR Report No. 43, paragraph 82.

was not a bar to promotion. Anglia Building Society operated a company-wide promotion policy and this led the Commission to conclude that if a unit had been recommended in this case it would have been a company-wide unit. One of the factors telling against a unit including managers in a number of Parsons "Working Arrangements" was that there was no common career pattern between these different areas of employment.*

Recruitment source

151. One reason for recommending the Acton unit for Horizon Holidays and its related companies' staff was that employees were locally recruited for these offices.†

(vi) The views of employers and trade unions

152. The Commission has always given careful consideration to the views of employers and trade unions when determining bargaining unit questions. This is because the boundaries of units must be acceptable to the parties if they are to be viable and provide long-run stability. Generally the boundaries of bargaining units have been those wanted by the unions recommended for recognition or have at least been acceptable to them.‡ Employer wishes were met in about half of the references.

Employer arguments

153. Arguments put forward by employers on the desired shape of bargaining units have been based on three main objectives. Companies have wanted to exclude various levels of management from units; to relate units to what they consider to be appropriate organisational boundaries; and to prevent the fragmentation of the workforce.

154. In most cases managers have not been included in the scope of a reference or have been excluded from a bargaining unit by mutual agreement. The arguments used by employers for the exclusion of managers have not therefore been reported in detail. It can however be assumed that the reasons given by the CIR for excluding managerial groups from the units for employees they supervised, such as in Parsons and Bridgwater Building Society, are broadly in line with company views. In general these reasons have included distinct job responsibilities, especially management responsibilities; methods of determining pay and conditions; existing collective bargaining arrangements; and the preferences of those in the managerial groups.

155. Employer arguments have been reported most often where the issue involved has concerned the organisational extent of a unit since companies have been anxious that recommended units should accord with their own

---

*CIR Report No. 32, paragraph 56.
†CIR Report No. 43, paragraph 75.
‡See Appendix II for the views of employers and trade unions regarding bargaining units in each reference.

organisation. This has sometimes meant favouring units which cover the whole of an organisation but in others units restricted to a part of an organisation have been preferred.

156. Two examples of companies presenting arguments in favour of organisation-wide units were William Hill and Munden. The company arguments were accepted in the first case but not in the second. William Hill argued that there was a decision-making structure in the company for labour relations matters and that the group was responsible for conditions of employment, there were group-wide procedures and a common wage-payment system was proposed.* Since there was also narrow majority support for collective bargaining in each of the four divisions of the company and a clear overall majority of support among employees, the CIR accepted these arguments.

157. The CIR was asked by the company, Equity Enterprises, to consider proposing an extension of the scope of the Munden reference to include the Sherman group, another part of the company based in South Wales.† Four arguments were presented in support of this suggestion:

(i) there was centralised control of all betting interests at Equity Enterprises' London head office;

(ii) although wage rates differed between the two groups other terms and conditions were common;

(iii) the company wanted to avoid the development of fragmented arrangements; and

(iv) the company wanted one union for all its staff which would be the same despite the expansion of the company.

Various factors were taken into account in considering the proposal of which probably the most important was that Equity Enterprises was responsible only for overall financial and expansion policy. The day-to-day management of the betting interests rested with the managements of the two betting groups and terms and conditions of employment were also substantially different between them. The CIR did not consider that it was necessary to propose an extension of the reference.

158. Barclays International was anxious to retain its autonomy from Barclays Bank‡ and argued in favour of bargaining units which would be separate from any arrangement involving "Limited". The main arguments presented by the company were that the trading activities of Barclays International differed from those of Barclays Bank and that terms and conditions of employment were also distinct. These arguments, supported by the other factors, were accepted by the CIR.

---

*CIR Report No. 63, paragraph 39.
†CIR Report No. 74, paragraph 21.
‡CIR Report No. 58, paragraph 34.

159. Seymour and Story was an unusual reference in that the management of a centralised company wanted their organisation to be subdivided for bargaining purposes. The company contended that two bargaining units, in one of which it negotiated with a Yorkshire Staff Committee, and in the other, with a Lancashire Committee, would be adequate. To support this, the company argued that the job content of Yorkshire employees was less sophisticated than in Lancashire and was therefore less well-paid. Lancashire employees also had a wider range of work and a slightly longer week.* These considerations should lead to separate units, it was argued. The CIR did not make recommendations in this case but had it done so it is doubtful whether the differences in job content and terms and conditions of employment would have led to separate units.

160. Pan American and Airline Engineering raised similar issues. The first problem was whether licensed aircraft engineers should be grouped in a unit with unlicensed aircraft engineers. The second problem was whether, if one unit were recommended for all aircraft engineers, the scope of this unit should be further extended to incorporate other groups of employees. These groups included non-aircraft mechanics and stock clerks in Pan American and back-up technicians employed by Airline Engineering. The company in both cases wanted one unit for all aircraft engineers. Pan American argued that such a unit would prevent friction amongst the employees who were an "essentially cohesive group".† Neither company was sympathetic towards the special position of licensed aircraft engineers and both emphasised the similar nature of the jobs, the experience and the similar backgrounds of the licensed and unlicensed grades.

161. In both these references the company view on the position of licensed engineers was accepted by the CIR although proposals concerning other groups were not. The management case for including non-aircraft mechanics and stock clerks in the Pan American unit was accepted because it would help to simplify the conduct of negotiations and minimize potential friction between employees. Furthermore, a single unit, Pan American contended, would not be detrimental to aircraft maintenance and safety standards.

162. The management of Airline Engineering wanted a group of technical back-up staff included in a unit which would allow existing arrangements to continue, and, the company argued, would be appropriate, since all the employees including the back-up staff, had similar training and backgrounds. They were also all concerned with the maintenance of aircraft.

---

*CIR Report No. 64, paragraphs 8 and 23.
†CIR Report No. 55, paragraph 58.

163. The CIR recommended a unit in line with the company views in Pan American but the recommendation was also based on other grounds including majority support for such a unit among the employees concerned. The company case for including the technical back-up staff of Airline Engineering was not however accepted. The CIR decided that in their training, qualifications and experience this group was different from the aircraft engineers. Furthermore there was strong opposition among aircraft engineers to continuing with bargaining arrangements in which they were included with back-up staff.

*Trade union arguments**
164. Trade union arguments in support of particular bargaining units have generally been based on their recruitment policies. In some cases the policy has been to recruit and represent exclusive or restricted groups of employees because of similar occupation or a single employer.

165. The ALAE presented two main arguments in favour of separate bargaining units for licensed engineers employed by Pan American and Airline Engineering. These were that licensed engineers formed a distinct group because of their training and their technical and statutory responsibilities. These arguments therefore related to job content and qualifications. It was argued that since existing bargaining arrangements did not take into account the different interests of the licensed group, the result was a "loss of personal esteem, job satisfaction and favourable pay differentials."† The ALAE went on to contend that the licensed mechanics' job involved a high degree of skill which was only acquired after rigorous formal training and significant private study. A special point was made of the licensed engineers' responsibility for air safety.

166. Both NALHM and the BBSA put forward arguments in support of company or group-wide units as opposed to units for subsidiary "management companies". NALHM contended that a recommended unit should cover public house managers in the whole of Allied Breweries because they had a common employer (contracts of employment named Allied Breweries); they were all doing the same work; and all shared in a common "professionalism"‡ The BBSA favoured a unit linking Barclays Bank with Barclays International, because, it argued, there were common conditions of employment, and staff transfers took place between the two companies.§

167. The argument presented by UKAPE to support its preferred unit in Parsons is reported only briefly. UKAPE are reported as arguing that qualified engineers had a community of interest but there is no indication of what was meant by this or the factors that these common interests might be based on.||

---

*Defined to include staff associations.
†CIR Report No. 55, paragraph 64.
‡CIR Report No. 38, paragraph 66.
§CIR Report No. 58, paragraph 57.
||CIR Report No. 32, paragraph 69.

168. Trade union arguments have usually attempted to persuade the CIR to recommend units which suit the organising philosophy of the union concerned. Two of these unions, ALAE and UKAPE, have an organisational philosophy based on qualifications or concepts of professionalism which would produce unions restricted to relatively narrowly-defined categories of employee in a limited range of industries. For these unions to be recognised by employers separately from other unions, bargaining units would have to be restricted to the groups of employees organised by these unions.

169. The BBSA also had a restricted recruitment policy since it wished to take into membership all non-management employees of the wider Barclays organisation. For organisations such as this to have bargaining independence and for bargaining units to meet with their wishes these units have to be organisation-wide. These "common-employer" unions are also opposed to the fragmentation of units which may provide openings for recruitment by unions which have wider organisational and recruiting policies.

170. The willingness of unions based on restricted organisational philosophies to argue in favour of particular units is rooted deeply in the purpose of their organisations. These unions believe that their continued credibility if not their existence depends on their ability to secure bargaining units which accord with their organising policies and which enable them to maintain their membership. If even small numbers of the employees they wish to represent are organised and represented in separate units and by other unions then their arguments for distinctive representation and organisation are threatened.

(vii) Summary

171. In the determination of a bargaining unit a number of closely-associated problems arise. The work groups which could be included in a unit have to be identified. Next the core of a unit has to be identified and this core may consist of one work group or two or more groups associated together. Finally, after a core has been identified, it may be decided to extend it further by including additional work groups. In practice, the second and third stages may be indistinguishable.

172. When decisions are made about which work groups could form the cores of units and the extent of possible units, four basic issues arise. These concern the potential organisational, vertical, horizontal and geographical extents of the work groups and possible bargaining units.

173. The CIR determined the extent of units by reference to a large number of factors. Some such as job skills and content; other conditions of employment; payment systems; attitudes to bargaining; and employee preferences of association helped to determine many issues but others arose infrequently.

174. It should not be assumed that because a factor was relevant in many issues, it was always important. Some factors which were relevant in only a minority of issues were often very important when they did arise. Such factors included the maintenance of existing collective bargaining arrangements; the presence of management operated procedures; the training and experience of employees; management structure; and physical working conditions.

175. The value of the various factors is that they provide a guide to what may be important in particular references. It should not, however, be assumed that the factors can be assessed in terms of relative importance in isolation from the circumstances in which they arise since these vary from one case to another.

176. Nor do the views of the parties present conclusive reasons in favour of a particular unit although they are important for two reasons. First they help to clarify what factors are considered to be important. Second these views need to be taken into account if the recommendations are to be acceptable. Employers are usually concerned to exclude various levels of management from units for other employees; to relate units to what they consider to be appropriate organisational boundaries; and to prevent the fragmentation of work groups and negotiating arrangements. Trade unions generally prefer units which suit their own recruitment strategies especially if they restrict their activity to cover employees of particular employers or occupational groups.

3 The determination of bargaining agents

(i) Introduction

177. The Industrial Relations Act established three standards which had to be met by trade unions and staff associations if they were to be recommended for recognition as a bargaining agent.* These were standards of independence, support in a bargaining unit, and effectiveness.† However, the CIR was used to considering such issues before the Act came into existence and had wide experience of handling bargaining agent questions.

178. The Act stated that an "independent" union was one that was not employer dominated or controlled.‡ The level of support which an agent should have was to be "substantial" and "effectiveness" was related to the availability of "resources", although these were not specified.

179. The CIR had considerable scope for interpreting and applying these standards and so had to take decisions on a number of questions including:

(i) What are the essential features of "independence"?

(ii) How can "dependence" be recognised?

(iii) What form should "support" take and how it be assessed?

(iv) What levels of "support" are "substantial" and what are the general wishes of employees?

(v) What resources are required for "effectiveness"?

(vi) How can "effectiveness" and "potential effectiveness" be assessed?

180. The CIR had to decide these issues and interpretations of "support levels" "independence" and "effectiveness" emerged. It is therefore possible to make some generalisations about these standards and the way in which unions can satisfy them. Although not applicable to all situations, these generalisations can have considerable value as guidelines in the handling of recognition cases by third parties in the future.

---

*In the Act an unregistered trade union was called an "organisation of workers".
†Section 48 (4) (a); (5) (a); (5) (b), respectively.
‡Section 167 (1).

181. The Commission had already gained some experience of assessing these criteria in the 13 pre-Act recognition references which it handled. In these references 13 unions and staff associations claimed recognition to represent some or all of the employees in the referred companies. The Amalgamated Union of Engineering Workers (AUEW) and the Association of Scientific, Technical and Managerial Staff (ASTMS) each put forward claims to be recognised by three separate employers. There was one instance where four organisations were in competition—ASTMS, British Medical Association (BMA), Association of University Teachers (AUT) and the Association of the Medical Research Council Scientific and Technical Staff (AMRCSTS) in Medical Research Council. One reference concerned the conflicting claims of two organisations, ASTMS and the Commercial Union Group Staff Association (CUGSA), in Commercial Union. The remaining references concerned claims by a single union. The CIR recommended that a single organisation should be recognised for negotiating purposes in 10 of the references while a joint panel was suggested for Commercial Union. In two cases, Electric Windings and British Home Stores, the companies were recommended to grant representational rights with a view towards granting full recognition at a later date.

182. In this Chapter we also examine the way in which the criteria have been interpreted and applied in 23 of the post-Act recognition references which we examined. In these references 16 bodies which purported to be independent organisations of workers claimed recognition in over 30 possible bargaining units. Some of these organisations claimed to represent more than one unit, sometimes in more than one reference. For example, TUBE claimed eight units; NUBE claimed seven and ASTMS claimed four. In some cases consideration was given to recommending joint panels as possible agents (in Allied Breweries a joint panel was recommended). Seven unions were recommended for recognition in 18 units and eight failed to achieve recognition in any unit. Some organisations were unsuccessful because they lacked adequate support, others were not considered to be independent and effective or did not meet any of these standards. The seven successful organisations were NALHM (two units and a joint panel); ASTMS (three units); the AUEW (two units); NUBE (four units); TUBE (four units); TASS (one unit); and TGWU (one unit and a share in a joint panel). The rest of this Chapter is divided into two parts: in the first questions of employee support are examined; in the second independence and effectiveness are examined.

(ii) Support for the agent

183. The CIR has assessed three forms of employee support for a potential agent in a bargaining unit:

(i) the actual membership level of a potential agent;

(ii) the number of employees in the unit who would prefer to be represented by a potential agent, or would "support" its recognition;

(iii) the number of employees who would be prepared to join the union if it were to be recognised*.

In most cases these factors have been taken together in assessing support levels to build up as complete a picture as possible of both present support and of ways in which employee attitudes might change in the future. Consequently the CIR has not simply "counted heads" to measure employees' support for possible agents but has gathered information in various ways before making decisions concerning bargaining agents.

184. The aim of the CIR to build up as broad a picture of employees' attitudes as possible was developed in the pre-Act period. Of particular importance was the practice of assessing potential support for an agent if it were recognised rather than relying on existing membership as an indicator of support. This practice was derived from the CIR's role of encouraging the expansion of collective bargaining which could be frustrated if a policy was adopted of recommending recognition only when a majority of employees in a unit were union members†. One example of this approach arose in Elliots of Newbury‡. In this case the fully paid-up membership of the union, the National Union of Furniture Trade Operatives (NUFTO) amounted to only 20-25 per cent of the "potential field". However the Commission estimated from a sample survey that 70 per cent of the workers favoured recognition and would be willing to join the union if it were recognised. This assessment helped to determine the recommendation that NUFTO should be recognised. In the case of John Bamber's Kings Lynn works, although the membership of the AUEW amounted to only 40 per cent of the workforce, the Commissions' inquiry showed that 75 per cent would join the union if it were recognised. The Commission thus recommended that recognition should be granted§. The Commission recognised that employees were unlikely to join unions in substantial numbers, especially if the employer had been hostile to unionisation, before recognition was granted.

185. Another interesting pre-Act case in which the Commission assessed employee support levels was the Commercial Union reference.|| Two organisations were competing to represent the employees of the company.

---

*Levels of actual membership have been calculated by interviewing employees; by inspecting unions' records; and, if necessary, by card checks. The CIR has also employed a number of methods for assessing employees' attitudes including interviewing all members of potential bargaining units, where possible; and interviewing samples of employees where the membership of a unit is too large for all to be interviewed. Postal questionnaires have also been frequently used.

†The Commission's approach to recognition cases is discussed in Chapter 3 of the First General Report (CIR Report No. 9). Paragraphs 36 to 38 are especially relevant to the assessment of support for the agent.

‡CIR Report No. 6.

§CIR Report No. 28. It should be noted however that actual union membership amounted to a majority in a number of the early cases, such as W. Stevenson and Sons, Suttons Cornwall Limited. (CIR Report No. 3); BSR Limited (CIR Report No. 5); and Brocks' Fireworks Limited (CIR Report No. 7).

||CIR Report No. 16: Commercial Union Assurance Co. Limited. This reference is also discussed later in connection with the independence of the staff association.

These were the Union of Insurance Staffs (which later merged with ASTMS) and the CUGSA. The company had about 8,700 employees at the time of the inquiry and the Commission took a sample survey of 400 employees. The survey showed that 16 per cent of employees were members of the union and 66 per cent were members of the staff association. Five alternative forms of bargaining arrangements were put to employees. These were: negotiations by the staff association only; by the union only; joint negotiations; and a merger between the two bodies. The fifth alternative asked employees who favoured joint negotiations whether they preferred the negotiating panel to have equal representation by the union and the association or whether there should be proportional representation according to their membership levels*. The support levels for three of these alternatives were as follows:

(i) negotiations by the staff association only: 29 per cent in favour

(ii) negotiations by the union only: 15 per cent in favour

(iii) joint negotiations: 36 per cent in favour

186. A merger of the two bodies was favoured by 39 per cent and opposed by 45 per cent, opposition being slightly higher among staff association members. Of 36 per cent who favoured joint negotiations, 43 per cent preferred equal representation and 51 per cent preferred proportional representation.

187. In this case, the Commission made two recommendations. They were that in the short-term negotiations should be carried on jointly while in the long-term there should be a merger of the union and the association. These proposals accorded with the expressed preferences of the largest group of employees in the sample.

188. The Commission continued to assess employee support levels in bargaining units in three types of reference which it received under the Industrial Relations Act. These were:

(i) company procedural cases from the Secretary of State for Employment referred to the CIR under Section 121(1) which involved recognition problems;

(ii) references from the Industrial Court under Section 46;

(iii) references from the Industrial Court under Section 52.

189. One of the Section 121(1) "recognition" cases, the second General Accident reference, had a number of features in common with the earlier Commercial Union reference. Many of these features arose from developments which had taken place in the company between the publication of the first General Accident report in December 1969 and the middle of

---

*CIR Report No. 16, paragraphs 104 to 108. There was, in fact, a further alternative: separate negotiations by each body on behalf of its members but the CIR did not consider this to be a realistic form of negotiations in the circumstances of this case (paragraph 107).

1972 when the second inquiry took place*. Of these changes the most important was the formation of a staff association, Staff Association–General Accident (SAGA), for General Accident employees and the consequent competition between this organisation and ASTMS for membership and negotiating rights. When the CIR inquired into support levels for possible agents in the new situation both the staff association and ASTMS were found to have substantial support.

190. The CIR sent a questionnaire to the company's 8,316 employees below the level of assistant manager, i.e. the proposed bargaining unit, and received a response rate of 95 per cent. Of the respondents, 1,982 were ASTMS members, 2,987 were SAGA members and 38 were joint members. Employees were asked to indicate their preferences between three possible forms of representation: representation by ASTMS only; representation by SAGA only; and joint representation by ASTMS and SAGA. Employees were asked which of these choices they would prefer, which they would accept, and which they would reject. The results are given in Table 1.

Table 1: Attitudes of General Accident employees to possible forms of representation†

	prefer	accept	reject	NS/NR‡
Representation by ASTMS only	3,065	1,101	3,234	916
Representation by SAGA only	2,932	1,262	3,239	883
Joint representation by ASTMS and SAGA	590	3,662	3,056	1,008

191. From Table 1 it can be seen that there were considerable numbers both in favour and against sole representation by either ASTMS or SAGA. A recommendation in favour of sole negotiating rights for either body would therefore be unacceptable to a large minority. However, although few employees preferred representation by a joint panel, a large number would accept it; and a marginally smaller number would reject this solution than would reject the other alternatives. Consequently, the Commission supported an ASTMS proposal for joint working arrangements for an interim period, with a view to a merger of the two organisations within six to 12 months§.

192. In General Accident employee attitudes towards a possible merger of ASTMS and SAGA were assessed with the result that 40.1 per cent were found to be in favour and 34.5 per cent opposed, the rest were indifferent

---

*CIR Reports No. 2 and 52.
†CIR Report No. 52, Table 3.
‡Not stated or no response.
§CIR Report No. 52, paragraph 102.

or "did not know". In this case, employee attitudes towards a number of possible short and long-term solutions were assessed and emphasis was placed on their "acceptability", given the difficulty of meeting the first preferences of either SAGA or ASTMS members and supporters.

193. Another Section 121 (1) "recognition" case of interest was Colvern* where there were two bargaining units, one for the company's hourly-paid employees and another for the staff. The number of employees in each unit was 391 and 61 respectively. The union claiming recognition for hourly-paid employees was the Electrical, Electronic Telecommunication and Plumbing Union (EETPU) and its white-collar section the Electrical and Engineering Staff Association (EESA) for staff. The recommendation for the hourly-paid unit was straightforward: 58 per cent of the employees in the unit were members of the union, and 70 per cent wished to be represented by it. Furthermore those who were already members or who said they would join following recognition amounted to 78 per cent of those in the unit. The EETPU was therefore recommended as agent for the hourly-paid employees.

194. Support for EESA among Colvern staff employees was more confused. Of 47 people interviewed, eight were members of the union, while one was a member of another union. Of the 38 non-members, six said they would like to join the union but were either still considering the matter or had not been asked; six more said they would join if the union were recognised; 19 said they were opposed to joining trade unions; and seven said they had no view about trade union representation†. Thus there was only a narrow majority in support of the union in the unit as it was then constituted. However the CIR pointed out that some charge-hands were paid on an hourly basis and had been included in the hourly-paid unit. This constituted an anomaly since these employees did similar work to those in the staff unit. These chargehands should therefore be given staff status and transferred to the staff unit. Since many of these employees were union members such a move would lend support to the recommendation that the company should recognise EESA as the agent for the staff.

195. The majority of Section 46 references can be divided into two groups according to the level of support for the eventually-recommended agents. First there are the references where there was already a relatively high level of union membership. In these cases, potential membership would also be high. The second group of references are those where the actual membership of a union in the unit was low but potential membership was high. Where either of these situations existed, i.e. where there was at least high potential membership, recognition was recommended. Table 2 shows both types of references.

---

*CIR Report No. 67: Colvern Limited.
†CIR Report No. 67, paragraph 29.

196. In addition to the two groups shown in the Table, there is a third class, which might be described as "actual membership low, potential moderate". This group had one representative: ASTMS in Horizon Holidays. The actual membership in the unit at Acton stood at 34 per cent and the potential was 43 per cent, but recognition was recommended.

197. There are two references which cannot easily be classified according to actual and potential support levels and these are Allied Breweries and Barclays International. In Allied Breweries the Commission decided to recommend three bargaining units, one for each of the organisation's "management companies". Only actual union membership was taken into account in determining support levels. NALHM had high levels of membership in two divisions, Ind Coope and Joshua Tetley's, in which the levels of membership were 75 per cent and 81 per cent respectively; in these units NALHM was recommended as the agent. However, although NALHM also had a high level of membership in Ansells (62 per cent), 23 per cent. of the managers in this division were already TGWU members*. Consequently a joint panel of the two unions was recommended† The employees were asked whether they would accept this arrangement and 69 per cent agreed including 54 per cent of the NALHM members.

198. The CIR assessed the support levels of three groups of staff in Barclays International. A sample of 288 of the clerical and auxiliary staff were interviewed while questionnaires were sent to all of the technical and services staff and to all of the computer staff‡. Consequently it is not possible to give aggregate support totals for the potential agents in the unit as a whole. Two of the three groups, the technical and auxiliary service staff and the computer staff, displayed high levels of actual and potential membership of NUBE. Their actual membership percentages were 80 and 74 respectively. The corresponding potential membership percentages were 78 and 83.

Table 2: Support levels where recognition has been recommended—actual and potential union membership

	Union	Actual membership Per cent	Potential membership Per cent
High actual and high potential membership			
Pan-American	AUEW	67	78
Con Mech	AUEW	70-90	80
Gordon Nunns	TUBE	72	85
John Joyce	TUBE	65	81
Ken Munden	TUBE	51	80
Davenport Brewery	TGWU	46	66
Low actual but high potential membership			
Associated Octel	ASTMS	25	75
Coventry Economic B.S.	NUBE	39	61
Connor and Forbes	TUBE	42	70
Bridgwater B.S. (branch managers)	NUBE	30	81
Bridgwater B.S. (other staff)	NUBE	21	77
William Hill	TUBE	16	63

*CIR Report No. 38, paragraphs 95 to 98.
†CIR Report No. 38, paragraph 100.
‡CIR Report No. 58, paragraphs 78 to 88.

199. Among the clerical and auxiliary group of staff in the Barclays International unit actual membership of NUBE was 39 per cent. but membership potential was fairly high at 61 per cent.

200. In one reference, Parsons, it was not possible to precisely assess either actual or potential membership of the recognised agent, TASS, but actual membership was known to be high.

201. Various methods have been used to assess support for unions other than by membership or potential membership figures. For instance, employees of the Bridgwater Building Society were asked "How would you describe your attitude to the recognition of NUBE by the society to negotiate pay and conditions on your behalf?"* Another example is found in Munden where employees were asked "Which organisation, if any, would you wish to represent you in negotiations with the company about pay and conditions?"† Such inquiries help to provide information about employees' attitudes towards particular trade unions and to supplement information obtained about membership levels, and are therefore of considerable value as a guide to employee wishes on the question of collective representation. For this reason, employee attitudes towards unions have been obtained in a number of references. Table 3 gives examples of where this has been done and where the information has been used to support recognition recommendations. It should be noted that the totals are not strictly comparable since the form of the questions and the circumstances in which the questions were put varied.

Table 3: Employee attitudes to unions eventually recommended as a bargaining agent

	Union	Percent in favour
Connor and Forbes	TUBE	63.0
Pan American	AUEW	69.0
Bridgwater B.S. (branch managers)	NUBE	62.5
Bridgwater B.S. (other staff)	NUBE	55.5
Gordon Nunns	TUBE	72.0
Ken Munden	TUBE	78.0
Associated Octel	ASTMS	56.0
William Hill	TUBE	58.5
Davenport Brewery	TGWU	58.0

202. Employee preferences for possible agents as a factor has tended to support conclusions reached on the basis of trade union membership or potential membership. More employees have had favourable attitudes towards a recommended union than have actually been members of it. However more employees have stated that they would be prepared to join a union if it were recognised than have had a favourable attitude towards it.

203. Two cases slightly complicate the general picture. These are Coventry Economic and Horizon Holidays. In both Coventry Economic and Horizon

*CIR Report No. 57, Table 4.
†CIR Report No. 74, Table 3.

Holidays the level of support for the union eventually recommended as the agent was low. Employees of Coventry Economic were asked "whether or not you are a member of the staff association or NUBE, do you support one of them and if so which one?" and in response, only 40 per cent supported NUBE.* The unit at Acton in the Horizon Holidays reference included both supervisors and other staff. Each group was asked whether, if a trade union were recognised, they preferred to be represented by ASTMS, by another union, or whether they had no preference. Only 26 per cent in each group preferred ASTMS although there was no strong preference for another union.† 50 per cent stated that they had "no preference".

204. The decision to recommend NUBE in Coventry Economic therefore rested heavily on the 61 per cent who were potential or actual members. The Horizon Holidays unit had a substantial level of union membership— over 30 per cent—but 54 per cent were in favour of collective bargaining. The 26 per cent who favoured ASTMS as the agent was probably a poor indication of employee support since this figure was less than the total ASTMS membership in the unit. It is probable that this factor was discounted in the recommendation.

205. There are two main reasons why potential bargaining agents may not be recommended because of support level reasons. First a potential agent (single union or joint panel) may have less support than another potential agent. Second there may be situations where no agent has enough support to justify a recognition recommendation. In five references there were instances of unions or joint panels being rejected as agents in particular units in favour of other agents and there are seven instances of possible units where no union had enough support to secure recognition.

206. Table 4 lists potential agents which were unable to secure recognition although other organisations were able to do so.

Table 4: Potential agents which failed to obtain recognition (others being successful)

	Potential Agent	Actual membership *Per cent*	Potential membership *Per cent*	Favouring recognition *Per cent*
Coventry Economic B.S.	Staff association	54	58	50
Connor and Forbes	Leisure and General Staff Association (LGSA)	61	NA[1]	28
	Joint panel	—	—	1
Bridgwater B.S. (branch managers)	Managers' staff association	100	100	50
Bridgwater B.S. (other staff)	Staff association	100	100	22
Pan American	ALAE	22	NA	NA
Barclays International: (clerical)[2]	BBSA	25	NA	NA
(technical)[2]	BBSA	20	NA	NA
(computer)[2]	BBSA	60	NA	NA

[1]Not available   [2]Groups within the unit

*CIR Report No. 42, paragraph 75.
†CIR Report No. 43, Table 5.

207. One agency possibility is not reflected in Table 4. The clerical and auxiliary group of employees of Barclays International were asked for their views on negotiation by a joint committee of NUBE and the BBSA. This suggestion was supported by 50 per cent but 28 per cent were against. Among computer staff there was 36 per cent support for a joint panel.

208. In Connor and Forbes the alternatives to TUBE as a bargaining agent clearly lacked support* and in the Bridgwater reference the staff association was considerably less well supported as a bargaining agent when compared with NUBE.†

209. In the Barclays International case the situation was complicated because actual BBSA membership gave the impression that it was well supported among the computer staff but many of these were also members of NUBE and 76 per cent of them favoured NUBE as a sole representative (see paragraph 207). The apparent indifference of the clerical group towards NUBE was also modified when the potential membership level of the organisation is taken into account. Adequate support for NUBE in the unit was finally suggested by the firmer support for the union and lack of interest in the staff association among technical staff.‡ The recommendation for NUBE rather than the BBSA or a panel can therefore be seen to rest on support criteria.

210. The managers of the Bridgwater Building Society's offices were evenly divided on the question of continued recognition for their own organisation. However some were already members of NUBE, a majority were in favour of recognition of that union and a large majority would remain members or would join the union if it were recognised. The recognition of NUBE was therefore strongly supported despite support for the continuance of existing arrangements.

211. In general where there is competition between possible agents for recognition consideration of various measures of support and potential support often reveals a union which will be a viable agent. An exception to this was Coventry Economic where support was divided between NUBE and a staff association (Table 5). It can be seen that only on potential membership after recognition had been secured did either organisation show a clear majority of support so that no firm conclusions could be reached on support levels alone.

Table 5: Support levels in Coventry Economic

	Actual membership Per cent	Potential membership Per cent	Favouring recognition Per cent
NUBE	39	61	40
Staff association	54	58	50

*CIR Report No. 44, Table 2.
†CIR Report No. 47, Table 3.
‡CIR Report No. 58, paragraphs 81, 86 and 88.

212. In six of the references where no agent was recommended in a possible unit there was inter-union or union-staff association competition which was largely responsible for the employees concerned being left unrepresented.* The references are Parsons (staff above the assistant manager line); Barclays International (board-appointed staff); and Seymour and Story, Anglia Building Society, Norwich Union and Hector Macdonald (all employees). Support levels for the competing potential agents in these cases are given in Table 6. Norwich Union is of particular interest because the two potential agents, with the help of the Commission, came to an agreement that negotiating rights in the company would be shared for a period of 12 months while a merger was arranged. However, when a ballot was held of the members of the two organisations on the question of whether they accepted this agreement, there was a low response rate. ASTMS members were heavily in favour but only 25 per cent. of Norwich Union Group Staff Association (NUGSA) members favoured the agreement and almost as many opposed it. NUGSA therefore felt unable to pursue these proposals preferring to wait for the publication of the Commission's report before taking further action. Although the Commission was unable to make any formal recommendations the report pointed out that the agreement reached by the two organisations would provide the best possible solution in the circumstances.

Table 6: Support levels where no agent was recommended because of union competition.

	Union	Actual membership *Per cent*	Potential membership *Per cent*	Favouring recognition *Per cent*
C. A. Parsons (above the line)	UKAPE	19	54	NA[1]
	ASTMS	7	53	NA
	TASS	7	NA	NA
Barclays International (board-appointed staff)	NUBE	28	44	39
	BBSA	41	48	few
	Joint panel	—	—	25
Seymour and Story	TUBE	29	52	37
	Staff committees	37	NA	51
Anglia Building Society	ABSSA	53	64	43
	NUBE	16	36	17
	Joint panel	—	—	12
Norwich Union	NUGSA	33	48	52
	ASTMS	22	37	43
	Joint panel	—	—	49
Hector Macdonald	TUBE	8	38	22
	Staff association	27	NA	50

[1]Not available

213. Union membership above the line in Parsons was divided between unions which were unlikely to agree on a joint panel. Both the main

*This needs to be qualified to the extent that some staff associations may have had adequate support but were not independent.

tenders had similar potential support levels and neither union seemed capable of achieving a clear majority of members even if it were recognised,* although there was "evidence of a degree of interest" in collective bargaining.†

214. There was even less likelihood of majority membership for a single union representing board-appointed staff in Barclays International. Even if recognised neither the union nor the staff association would have been able to recruit a majority in the unit.

215. The Seymour and Story staff were sharply divided between supporters of the union (TUBE) and the staff committees and these divisions would prevent a recognised organisation from securing substantial support.‡ The same can be said about the Anglia situation, especially as the membership of NUBE was concentrated in Northampton.

216. In these cases although units might have been established and where majorities might have favoured collective bargaining the division of membership and potential membership between competing organisations prevented bargaining agent recommendations being made by CIR.

217. Finally, no recommendations were made in the Airline Engineering and Temperance Building Society cases although there was only one candidate for recognition in the units. The failure of the ALAE in Airline Engineering arose because an exclusive union or by seeking to represent engineers with a specialist qualification only two-thirds of the employees in the possible unit were eligible for membership.§ The CIR felt that a union could not be recognised unless all employees in the unit were eligible for membership that it would not be realistic to assess employee support levels in the usual way and that the union should reconsider its membership policy.

218. The Temperance reference is one of the few in which a union failed to obtain recognition although not competing with another union.‖ There were two possible units in this case and the support levels for the union, NUBE, were as shown in Table 7. Potential membership levels of little more than 30 per cent were found for the union, TUBE, in the Roland Jones and Ken Hailes references and so no recommendations were made.

Table 7: Support levels for NUBE in the Temperance Building Society.

	Actual membership Per cent	Potential membership Per cent	Favouring recognition Per cent
Managers	5	32	16
Other staff	16	35	31

*CIR Report No. 32, paragraph 74.
†CIR Report No. 32, paragraph 75.
‡CIR Report No. 64, paragraphs 29 to 32.
§CIR Report No. 66, paragraph 61.
‖CIR Report No. 75, paragraphs 45 to 48.

219. Union recognition on the basis of employee support levels has generally been recommended under three sets of circumstances. This does not mean that recognition will always be granted in these circumstances because questions of independence and effectiveness also have to be taken into account. The circumstances are:

(i) where the union has a clear majority of actual members in a unit recognition will be granted;

(ii) where a union without a majority of members in a unit has a reasonable majority favouring it (sometimes in preference to another body) and has high potential membership it is likely to secure a recognition recommendation. It is unlikely to secure recognition if there is considerable hostility to it among employees in the unit;

(iii) where two organisations have substantial levels of actual or potential members a joint negotiating panel may be recommended. However full recognition may not be possible in which case limited representation rights may be recommended.

220. Independent and effective unions with a membership of 60 per cent in a unit have been in a strong position to be recognised. Unless there is a very high level of dual membership such unions dominated a situation. However, there may be another union present with a substantial minority membership, e.g. 20-30 per cent. Such a union could be included in a joint panel e.g. the TGWU in Allied Breweries (Ansells division).

221. A union with membership of less than 20 per cent might be recommended for recognition if potential membership was in the region of 60 per cent provided there was no strong opposition to it. Recognition was recommended for TUBE in William Hill where actual membership stood at 16.4 per cent for this reason. Similarly, NUBE was recommended for the "other staff" unit of the Bridgwater Building Society with only 21 per cent membership. There was a competitor organisation in this case but it was not considered independent and effective.*

222. Some organisations have fallen short of minimum support levels to secure recognition in non-competitive situations. A membership level of 16 per cent with a potential of 35 per cent among other staff in the Temperance Building Society and the levels attained in the Ken Hailes, Roland Jones and Anglia Building Society cases were not considered adequate to support collective bargaining.

223. In cases where two potential agents have substantial support, with potential membership in the region of 40 to 60 per cent, no recommendations were possible. The only feasible arrangements, joint panels, were ruled out by the hostility between the aspiring agents or, in Seymour and Story, because the staff committees were not independent and effective. In these cases employee preferences for possible agents have not helped to clarify a situation.

---

*A staff association.

224. Another group of references added to the Commissions' experience of assessing employee support levels. These were the references made under Section 52 of the Act. These references followed an application to the Court by a group of employees who wanted an employer to cease recognising an existing bargaining agent. The Act provided for the CIR to conciliate in these cases but if conciliation failed to achieve a settlement then a ballot was conducted to determine whether the existing agent should continue to be recognised.

225. Bargaining units were specified in these references so that bargaining unit issues did not normally arise. However, in one case, National Coal Board Bulk Terminal, Immingham, the CIR found the initial unit to be too small.* The reference had covered only non-craft manual employees but, at the Commissions' request, the scope of the reference was extended to include a number of craftsmen.

226. Generally these references have concerned bargaining agents. In two of these references NAAFI and Pfizer Limited,† members of the bargaining units were asked which agent they preferred to represent them. In the NAAFI reference, the bargaining unit consisted of senior clerical officers and junior managers who were represented by the Junior Management Staff Association (JMSA). The alternative agent was ASTMS which had 138 of the 712 employees in membership. 35 per cent said they preferred ASTMS and 40 per cent preferred the JMSA. When conciliation failed to produce a solution a ballot was held and the result was 332 votes against the continued recognition of the JMSA, and 282 in favour.

227. The Pfizer reference arose from an application by a number of employees in a bargaining unit consisting of laboratory technicians and assistants, computer operators and draughtsmen to have recognition withdrawn from a Weekly Paid Staff Consultative Committee (WPSCC). The employees constituted "Group 1" of four groups represented by this body. Again ASTMS had recruited in the bargaining unit and was an alternative representative to the WPSCC. The Commission found that 12 per cent of the 219 employees in the unit were members of ASTMS and a further 39 per cent of those interviewed indicated that they would be willing to join ASTMS if it were recognised by the Company for bargaining purposes.‡ When they were asked whom they wished to negotiate pay and conditions of employment on their behalf, 49 per cent preferred their group's representatives on the consultative committee, 28 per cent preferred ASTMS, and nine per cent a joint panel of the two organisations. This relatively strong support for the existing arrangements was later reflected in the results of a ballot. Of the 200 who voted, 160 were in favour of continued recognition of the WPSCC and 40 voted against the continued recognition of this body.

---

*CIR Report No. 41: National Coal Board Bulk Terminal, Immingham.
†CIR Report No. 60: Navy, Army and Air Force Institutes (NAAFI), and CIR Report No. 61: Pfizer Limited.
‡79 employees were interviewed.

(iii) Independence and effectiveness

228. "Independence" and "effectiveness" are closely related but distinct concepts. The essence of "independence" is freedom from employer influence while "effectiveness" relates to the ability to organise and maintain membership and to represent members to their employers. "Independence" is therefore a pre-condition of effectiveness, especially for the representational function. Unions cannot effectively represent their members if they are employer-dominated so they must have a minimum level of independence. But although "effectiveness" requires some degree of independence there can be no presumption that an independent body will be effective.

229. There are therefore two questions which can be asked about potential agents in connection with their independence and effectiveness:

(i) Is the organisation "independent"?

(ii) Is an independent organisation "effective"?

230. If the answer to question (i) is "yes", then it is possible to ask question (ii), if the answer to question (i) is "no" it is meaningless to ask the second question: a "dependent" organisation is by definition "ineffective." There are therefore three possible verdicts which may be passed on an aspiring agent:

(a) It is dependent.

(b) It is independent but ineffective.

(c) It is independent and effective.

231. Trade unions may demonstrate their independence and effectiveness in many ways, for instance by membership of the TUC and other trade union federations, by political action and a willingness to take some form of industrial action in pursuit of members' interests. A history of vigorous negotiations resulting in reasonable settlements also suggests independence and effectiveness. However borderline cases have to be examined in the light of a number of criteria. Most of the criteria used to test independence differ in character from the criteria used to test effectiveness. Evidence of independence comes from examining the history of an organisation to discover the part played by employers in establishing it and their influence on the way it has developed and operates. Effectiveness concerns behaviour and in particular the way in which an organisation acts and reacts to its surroundings; the resources it has to formulate and implement its policies; and the results it achieves.

232. From the concepts of independence and effectiveness criteria can be derived to assess particular organisations. It should be emphasised that these criteria form guidelines only since no organisation will be independent and effective according to all the criteria. Two other points also need to be made. First the criteria have to be applied in a realistic and flexible manner. For example, although an independent organisation should not depend on management, allowance must be made for the fact

that one way in which a union might enforce a closed shop is by means of management support. Although a closed shop may have advantages for management, maintaining a closed shop established as result of pressure from an independent trade union should be distinguished from forcing employees into membership of a management-dominated "house" union. An examination of each of the criteria will reveal the need for a flexible approach along these lines. The second point to be made regarding the use of the independence and effectiveness criteria is that they have to be applied in dynamic situations. Many of the more complex problems concerning independence and effectiveness which have faced the CIR have concerned bodies in the process of changing from a dependent to an independent situation. Other problems have concerned bodies which were ineffective at the time of the inquiry but which might become effective if appropriate steps were taken. Consequently in the use of the criteria attention has had to be paid not only to the current situation but also to the possibility of a dependent and ineffective organisation becoming independent and effective in the near future. If such changes were likely to take place then the Commission could recommend that an organisation should be recognised subject to certain conditions.

233. Criteria of independence and of effectiveness include:

(a) *Independence*

(i) management should not be involved in the formation and running of the organisation;

(ii) financial support from management should not be essential to its continued existence;

(iii) membership should not depend on coercive or intimidatory measures by management;

(iv) meetings should not be attended by management except by invitation;

(v) there should be no obligation to submit minutes or to supply other confidential information to management;

(vi) management should not influence policy other than by the normal processes of negotiation;

(vii) there should preferably be a membership base outside the company;

(viii) the organisation should employ its own officials; and

(ix) the organisation should not be solely dependent on facilities afforded by management.

(b) *Effectiveness*

(i) the organisation should have adequate income for representational purposes and negotiations;

(ii) there should be sufficient experienced and/or trained officials;

(iii) the structure of the organisation should be adequate and appropriate for the employees in the unit;

(iv) it should have access to research, legal and other necessary expertise;

(v) there should be a satisfactory record of:

(a) maintaining membership;

(b) representing and servicing members; ✓

(c) negotiating and concluding agreements.

234. Taking the two categories of criteria together the CIR has found three types of organisations:

(i) those which were independent and effective;

(ii) those which were dependent on an employer;

(iii) a number of organisations whose independence or effectiveness was in doubt and therefore needed to be carefully assessed.

235. The organisations which were independent and effective required little examination. The qualifications of these bodies needed to be re-affirmed only briefly in reports. For example, TASS in Parsons was stated to be "an independent organisation of workers which has the resources and organisational capacity to represent effectively employees in the specified bargaining unit and has demonstrated its capacity to do so."* Similar affirmations were sufficient for the TGWU (Allied Breweries); NUBE (Coventry Economic and Bridgwater Building Societies); ASTMS (Horizon Holidays and Associated Octel); and the AUEW (Con Mech and Pan American).

236. It was recorded in the Pan American report that the AUEW had extensive experience of bargaining on behalf of aircraft maintenance employees; that the employees in the unit were impressed by the union's negotiating ability; and that the union had recently concluded an agreement with the firm which would enable services to be provided effectively to members.† Effectiveness in this case was therefore explicitly related to employees covered by the reference.

237. Bodies which were clearly not independent included the staff association of the Coventry Economic Building Society, the Leisure and General Staff Association in Connor and Forbes and the two staff committees established in Seymour and Story. Each of these bodies failed to meet many or all of the criteria outlined above.

---

*CIR Report No. 32, paragraph 71.
†CIR Report No. 55, paragraph 88.

238. The staff association in Coventry Economic may be taken as a typical example of this group. Senior management played an active part in the formation of the association, attending and speaking at staff meetings when the question of staff representation and the formation of an association were being discussed.* The general manager and his deputy applied for membership and 18 senior managers were still members at the time of the CIR inquiry. Four out of five of the committee members were head office managers who would be likely to experience conflict between their managerial and representational roles. There were no paid officials of the association and it was also dependent on interest-free loans made to it by senior managers. Such a body was not independent nor could it be expected to become independent.

239. Bodies like the Coventry Economic Staff Association were seen by management as alternatives to trade unions. In the Connor and Forbes case this was explicitly stated in a letter by management to their employees who were told that a staff association could expect the full co-operation of management.†

240. The Commission also came across an example of a body which was neither independent nor effective in the Williams and Glyn's reference. This was a reference under Section 121 of the Act where one of the main issues was the form which employee representation should take, with NUBE and the Williams and Glyn's Staff Association (WGSA) competing for recognition. The staff association failed to meet many of the criteria of independence and effectiveness. It had no paid officials and its officers were all full-time employees of the bank. Subscriptions had not been collected for two years and the level of actual membership was not known. Furthermore, membership was largely restricted to the old Glyn Mills branches where the association had originally been formed. Finally the likely effectiveness of the body in negotiations was further reduced by the fact that it had withdrawn from membership of the Council of Bank Staff Associations. As a negotiating body the WGSA would not therefore be strengthened by outside support.

241. There have been a number of bodies whose independence or effectiveness was in question but which were recommended as agents by the CIR subject to specific conditions being made. One example was found in the Commercial Union reference a pre-Act case which concerned the CUGSA. Another body which was examined was the staff association of General Accident employees (SAGA) in the second General Accident reference. The remainder arose from Section 46 references and the bodies concerned included NALHM (Allied Breweries) and TUBE (Connor and Forbes, William Hill and other references). Only the effectiveness of NALHM and TUBE was in doubt.

---

*CIR Report No. 42, paragraph 65.
†CIR Report No. 44, paragraph 54.

242. The constitution of the CUGSA had been influenced by the report of an inquiry by Lord Cameron* into the independence of bank staff associations. This report followed a complaint by NUBE that some banks were infringing the ILO Convention No. 98 on the freedom of association of employees by establishing bodies which were dependent on management. Although the inquiry did not find that these allegations had been proven, a number of points were made which were taken into account by the CUGSA in reforming its constitution†. In particular, a clause requiring management to consent to changes in the constitution was eliminated and membership was made voluntary and dependent on payment of subscriptions. The right of membership was extended to management above the level of superintendent but most senior executives were excluded. The new constitution also provided the basis for increased effectiveness by establishing a structure of committees for policy-making and the administration of the association's business. Furthermore an agreement was concluded with the company which provided for independent arbitration in the event of a failure to agree between the company and the association. The association pointed out to its members that this agreement introduced an element of independent bargaining for the first time in its relationship with the company.‡

243. In contrast to these movements towards greater independence and effectiveness a number of other factors pointed in the opposite direction. One of the most important of these was the low level of subscriptions, ranging from 25p to 60p a year. As a result the association was able to pay only 20 per cent of its general secretary's salary, the rest of which was paid by the company.§ The association was also dependent on the company for financial and other assistance. For instance, the company paid the salary of a full-time secretary to the general secretary; provided a fully-equipped office for the general secretary; gave the use of company premises for meetings; and provided various facilities for organising and communication with members.

244. The CIR decided that although the CUGSA lacked some of the requirements of an independent and effective body, the company had not attempted to dominate the organisation or to influence its officers. In the judgement of the Commission, these officials were "conscientious and competent people who, in general, have a clear understanding of the distinctions between their members' interests and those of the company, as well as the overlapping of those interests."‖ The association had recently achieved important settlements with management concerning salary increases and job evaluation as well as regularly handling individual members' problems and grievances. These impressions were confirmed by the general satisfaction expressed by members of the way in which the association had represented them.

---

*CMNd 2202, Stationery Office, 1963.
†CIR Report No. 16, paragraph 25.
‡CIR Report No. 16, paragraph 26.
§CIR Report No. 16, paragraph 41.
‖CIR Report No. 16, paragraph 98.

245. The Commission therefore recommended that the CUGSA should participate in a joint panel with ASTMS while taking steps to ensure its independence and effectiveness in the future.* The most important of these steps would be to become financially independent of the company and to pay the salaries of its general secretary and other full-time officials. This would clearly demonstrate the responsibility of the officials to the members and the independence of the organisation.†

246. The doubts about independence and effectiveness of SAGA were not resolved at the time of the CIR report partly because this body had its origins in staff committees set up on management initiative. Also important was the fact that it had only recently been formed and had not had time to prove its independence or effectiveness. One point which raised doubts about the organisation's independence was the assertion that management had promised to recognise it before it was established although this was denied by the association. The level of membership contributions, 25p to 30p per month, was also relatively low and the rival claimant for recognition, ASTMS, argued that this gave SAGA an unfair advantage in recruiting. The low level of subscriptions was reflected in the limited range of services provided by SAGA to its members. These did not include dispute benefits, benevolent grants or legal aid.

247. A number of factors were set against these impressions. Chief of these was the fact that the CIR found no evidence of any financial assistance or other subsidy from the General Accident Corporation to SAGA or of any other form of assistance or the provision of any facility which was not available to ASTMS. For example, management held parallel meetings with representatives of both bodies and provided both with check-off facilities. SAGA also paid an economic rent to the corporation and paid the salary of its own general secretary.

248. Only tentative recommendations were made in this case, partly because of the indecisive support levels and partly because neither body had had the opportunity to prove its effectiveness as the representative of General Accident employees. The CIR pointed out that SAGA in particular needed to define its main objective and to improve its organisation, particularly with regard to membership involvement and to increase its resources. However the hope was held out by the Commission that a body such as SAGA, which had started as a dependent body, might evolve into a fully-independent organisation capable of effective action.‡

---

*CIR Report No. 16, paragraph 108.

†CIR Report No. 16, paragraph 111.

‡In this case ASTMS was also found to be ineffective to some degree and there was a need for it to "review organisational efficiency and the performance and style needed to win wider support within the Corporation." (CIR Report No. 52, paragraph 119).

249. In Allied Breweries the TGWU raised doubts about the independence of NALHM because it was recognised by the Brewers' Society immediately on its formation. NALHM was however considered to be independent by the CIR on four grounds:
(i) it had received no financial assistance from employers during its formation;
(ii) the initiative to form NALHM had come from employees;
(iii) it had negotiated nationally and with individual companies as an independent trade union;
(iv) NALHM's income came solely from membership subscription.*

250. No serious challenge was made to the BBSA but there is always a need to assess the independence of staff associations which draw their membership from one employer. The CIR put forward a number of reasons why it considered that this association was independent.† It had been constituted as long ago as 1941 and was not formed in response to a recent campaign by a trade union. The association had a comprehensive branch, district and national structure with eight full-time officers. There was a total of over 23,000 members which enabled it to be self-financing and to employ 22 clerical staff. The association was also a party to the national clearing banks agreement. On various criteria therefore the BBSA was considered to be independent.

251. In the Connor and Forbes reference, both the independence and effectiveness of TUBE received close consideration but any doubts were dispelled after investigation. Doubts about independence were raised for two reasons: first during its formation TUBE had accepted £250 from a bookmaker and second a bookmaker had been one of the two honorary vice-presidents of the union. However the £250 was clearly marked in the union's accounts, the union was under no obligation to the donor and he was in no way involved in the union. The bookmaker who had been an honorary vice-president had withdrawn from the union.

252. Questions about TUBE's effectiveness in the Connor and Forbes reference arose because it was recognised by only nine small bookmaking chains for representational purposes alone and the union had no written agreements. These doubts were however allayed because the union had provided effective representation for individual and collective grievances and had also assisted members in Industrial Tribunal cases.

253. The doubts about TUBE were more pronounced in the William Hill reference. The number of the union's branches had fallen from 22 to eight; because of difficulties in collecting subscriptions its bank overdraft increased from £1,000 to £5,500 in 1973; and one of the three area officials had left the employment of the union. TUBE's membership and financial bases were therefore being rapidly eroded.

---

*CIR Report No. 38, paragraph 94.
†CIR Report No. 58, paragraphs 49 to 54.
‡CIR Report No. 63, paragraph 49.

254. The CIR decided that TUBE had not yet declined in effectiveness to the point where it should no longer be recognised at William Hill as a bargaining agent. The assurance of the union that the position could be reversed if it were recognised was accepted by the Commission which made its recommendation subject to the condition of TUBE putting its finances on a sounder footing and strengthening its organisation. These conditions included the requirement that for a period of three consecutive months the current monthly income of the union should exceed its current monthly expenditure. A second requirement was that the branches should appoint "collectors" to collect subscriptions and that arrangements should be made to collect subscriptions regularly by Giro arrangements or bankers' order. Third the Manchester and Glasgow branches should be reformed. Criteria of effectiveness were therefore given a concrete form in this case.

255. The staff associations in the Bridgwater Building Society are interesting because they were partially dependent on the employer but possessed some degree of autonomy. This element of autonomy permitted some effective bargaining despite the lack of funds, small size, and the absence of an independent base outside the company. The managers' association in particular was eager to argue that small size and lack of funds did not undermine independence or effectiveness. It argued that a small membership (16) made rapid communication possible without great expenditure. Furthermore the interest of the members in the association was shown by the high level of attendance at meetings. Effectiveness, it contended, was shown by the way it had negotiated a new salary structure for managers. The CIR did not accept the managers' arguments and took the view that neither the managers' association nor the "other staff" association was large enough to be able to develop and maintain necessary resources and organisation.

256. In practice independence is probably easier to establish than effectiveness because the criteria are clearer and because of the difference in the nature of the concepts. Taking criteria of independence first, the comparative clarity of the concept may be easily illustrated. Either the employer is involved in the administration of the organisation or he is not; he either provides it with funds or he does not; the organisation either has its own paid staff or it does not; and so on. Once the facts are available—and these may sometimes be difficult to obtain—the judgment is straightforward. For this reason, most institutions were seen to be independent or not after only a limited analysis and no prolonged inquiry was necessary. Even in a border-line case such as the BBSA an orderly application of the criteria produced an answer which was widely accepted by those covered by the reference.

257. Only in cases where a dependent organisation is in the process of transforming itself into an independent one are fine judgements necessary. In these cases, some criteria are likely to point to dependence while others will indicate independence. An example of such a case was the managers' association in the Bridgwater reference. On some criteria, such as the

absence of paid officials, restriction to one company and so on, there were obvious signs of dependence. However, other criteria, such as the absence of employer influence on policy-making pointed to a degree of independence. Although some bargaining had been founded on this independence long-term effectiveness was strongly doubted.

258. Criteria of effectiveness are more difficult to assess than those of independence. This is because there is less agreement on what constitutes an "effective" trade union than on what constitutes one which is independent. Some of the criteria may be used to illustrate the problems which could arise in their application. For example, no standard exists by which we can judge the financial resources a union needs to service a given number of members. Similarly, what is an "adequate" trade union structure in a given situation? The problem of relativity in criteria becomes even more acute in assessing effectiveness on the basis of performance. What are "satisfactory" agreements and what is a "satisfactory" record of representing members?

259. Some of the problems of interpreting criteria came up in connection with the effectiveness of TUBE. In these bookmaking references, reservations were made about the financial and administrative soundness of the organisation although recognition was recommended in several references. The reservation was that unless a clearer "demonstration" of effectiveness was achieved by the union on future occasions, it might not be judged "effective" again.

(vi) Concluding points

260. It has been a relatively straightforward matter to recommend the recognition of a trade union if it has most members of a bargaining unit in membership or has the potential of majority membership; if it is clearly independent; and if there is agreement on its effectiveness. Equally recognition can be refused to a body if it manifestly does not meet each of these standards.

261. Examination of CIR references has shown that the application of each standard in most references has not given rise to excessively complex problems. However some issues have arisen which have not been conclusively resolved. Some of the problems arise from the separate application of the three standards. Examples of this include:

(i) where majority support for a potential agent in a unit is slight, especially if there is strong minority opposition to the union.*;

(ii) where there are competing organisations which are well established in the unit and where mutual hostility prevents the recommendation of a joint panel†;

---

*NUBE in the Coventry Economic Building Society reference.

†UKAPE and its associates and ASTMS above the line in Parsons and NUBE and BBSA, for board-appointed staff, in Barclays International.

(iii) where the evidence concerning the independence of an organisation does not lead to a clear-cut decision*

(iv) where there is doubt about the effectiveness of an independent organisation.†

262. Difficult situations also arise when a dependent organisation satisfies the support level criteria in a unit. This happened in Seymour and Story where 51 per cent. of the employees favoured recognition of the staff committees.‡ These bodies were dependent on the employer, having been established for the purpose of providing an alternative to TUBE. Since only 37 per cent. of employees favoured the union this strategy seemed to have been successful.

263. There is also a problem of what should be done when a majority of employees favour an organisation which is clearly ineffective although the CIR has not had to consider this in an acute form. In this kind of situation, as Seymour and Story, there would be a conflict between granting employees what they want and what are realistic collective bargaining arrangements. The Commission certainly did not feel that these organisations should be endorsed by a third party with responsibility for encouraging effective collective bargaining.

264. Where there is marginal support for a union there is a strong argument in favour of recognition because once a union is recognised and seen to be accepted by an employer, employee support will develop and opposition from other employees will lessen. The act of recognition thus tends to bring about a significant change in employee attitudes. It takes time for these developments to take place and support to grow. Under these circumstances a premature ballot of employees would have limited value as a guide to whether recognition should be granted.

265. Where there are potential agents competing the parties seeking recognition can sometimes be helped by independent third party intervention. Normally hostile organisations may be reluctant to form a joint negotiating panel but this might be achieved if the parties see it is a better alternative to having no recognition at all. An important consideration in such cases is the strength of the belief that by pursuing competitive recruitment policies and continuing an uncertain situation one or other of the parties feels it might eventually secure sole negotiating rights.

266. Finally where an organisation's independence and effectiveness are in doubt they can sometimes be enhanced by securing recognition. A partially dependent organisation may achieve full independence under the

---

*The staff associations in the Bridgwater reference.
†TUBE in William Hill and other references.
‡See Table 6.

pressure of representative responsibilities and a union's effectiveness can be increased by extending the areas of employment in which it is recognised. However it must not be concluded that recognition should be extended to any applicant organisation because of dynamic considerations. Established independence and effectiveness should be given very high initial priority since, if an organisation fails to achieve these standards, employees will be left without adequate representation which could lead to further competitive recruitment and unstable collective bargaining arrangements.

Appendix I:
Pre-Act recognition references

Reference	The Associated Octel Company Limited	General Accident Fire and Life Assurance Corporation	W. Stevenson and Sons Suttons Cornwall Limited	BSR Limited	Elliots of Newbury Limited
Report No.	1	2	3	5	6
Date of reference	15 May 1969	15 May 1969	21 October 1969	21 October 1969	26 September 1969
Date of report	18 December 1969	31 December 1969	31 December 1969	11 February 1970	18 March 1970
Industry	Petrochemicals	Insurance	Fishing	Engineering	Furniture manufacture
Employees concerned in the recognition dispute	White-collar: supervisors and method improvement officers at Ellesmere Port	White-collar: managerial, supervisory and clerical	Fish-handlers and lorry drivers	Manual: production, maintenance and ancillary employees at East Kilbride	Manual: production, maintenance and ancillary employees
No. of employees concerned in the recognition dispute	126	9,460	Stevensons: 17 Suttons: 25	2,145	320
Type of establishment	Multi-establishment company	Multi-company, multi-establishment organisation	Single-establishment companies	Multi-establishment company	Single-establishment company
Unions and associations recommended to represent employees	ASTMS	UIS	TGWU	AUEW	NUFTO
Other unions and associations not recommended	None	None	None	None	None
Other information		The company was recommended to consult with but not, as yet, to negotiate with the union			

Reference	Brock's Fireworks Limited	Frederick Parker Limited	Medical Research Council	Commercial Union Assurance Company Limited	Electric Windings (London) Limited
Report No.	7	8	12	16	21
Date of reference	26 September 1969	5 December 1969	5 December 1969	14 May 1970	16 November 1970
Date of report	15 April 1970	10 June 1970	27 November 1970	20 April 1971	3 August 1971
Industry	Firework manufacture	Engineering	Medical research	Insurance	Electrical engineering
Employees concerned in the recognition dispute	Manual: production, maintenance and ancillary employees at Sanquhar, Dumfriesshire	White-collar: clerical	White-collar: non-clinical, scientific, technical officers and technicians	White-collar: managerial, supervisory and clerical	Manual employees at the Romford works
No. of employees concerned in the recognition dispute	370	216	2,300	8,700	250
Type of establishment	Multi-establishment company	Single-establishment company	Multi-establishment organisation	Multi-establishment company	Multi-establishment company
Unions and associations recommended to represent employees	GMWU	CAWU	ASTMS	Joint negotiating committee including CUGSA and ASTMS	None
Other unions and associations not recommended	None	None	BMA, AUT and AMRCSTS	None	None
Other information		The company should join the EEF which would entail recognition of the CAWU			The company was recommended to grant representational rights to EETU/PTU

73

Reference	British Home Stores	Engelhard Industries Limited	John Bamber Engineering Limited
Report No.	24	26	28
Date of reference	26 May 1970	16 November 1970	4 May 1971
Date of report	21 October 1971	11 January 1971	27 April 1972
Industry	Retail distribution	Chemicals	Engineering
Employees concerned in the recognition dispute	Employees at the Swansea store	Manual and staff "using engineering tools of the trade" at Cinderford	Manual employees
No. of employees concerned in the recognition dispute	The company: 12,266 Swansea: not available	60	171
Type of establishment	Multi-establishment organisation	Multi-national, multi-establishment company	Single-establishment company
Unions and associations recommended to represent employees	None	AUEW	AUEW
Other unions and associations not recommended	None	None	None
Other information	The company was recommended to grant representational rights to USDAW		

Appendix Ia:

Recognition references under Section 46, Industrial Relations Act 1971*

---

*This Appendix includes 23 references examined by the study team; it does not cover *all* Section 46 references received by the Commission.

75

Reference	C. A. Parsons and Co, Limited and associated companies	Allied Breweries (UK) Limited	Coventry Economic Building Society	Horizon Holidays Limited and associated companies	Connor and Forbes Limited
Report No.	32	38	42	43	44
Date of reference	1 March 1972	2 June 1972	6 December 1972	15 December 1972	18 January 1973
Date of report	16 October 1972	2 May 1973	19 July 1973	25 July 1973	2 August 1973
Origin of reference	Employer application	Application by NALHM	Application by NUBE	Application by Secretary of State for Employment	Application by TUBE
Industry	Electrical engineering	Public houses	Building society	Holiday travel	Betting offices
Type of employee	White-collar: technical staff	White-collar: public house and catering house managers	White-collar: managerial and clerical, some manual ancillary staff	White-collar: managerial, supervisory and clerical	White-collar: supervisory and clerical
No. of employees covered by reference	1,695	988	260	460	535
Type of establishment	Multi-company, multi-plant group	Multi-establishment company	Multi-establishment organisation	Multi-company, multi-establishment organisation	Multi-establishment company
Description of employees in recommended unit(s)	Technical staff below the level of assistant manager (the "line")	1. Managers in Ind Cooper division 2. Managers in Joshua Tetley division 3. Managers in Ansells division	All staff below the level of head office departmental manager and surveyor	Supervisors and staff of Horizon Holidays, Horizon Travel and 4S Travel employed at the Acton offices	All employees up to and including area managers, full-time managers and regular part-time
No. in unit(s)	1,431	1. 635 2. 876 3. 988	240	301	209
Recommended agent(s)	TASS	1. NALHM 2. NALHM 3. Joint panel: NALHM/TGWU	NUBE	ASTMS	TUBE
Other possible agents	UKAPE, APST, ASEE, ASTMS	None	None	None	LGSA

Reference	Con Mech (Engineers) Limited	Pan-American World Airways Incorporated	The Bridgwater Building Society	Barclays Bank International Limited	Messrs. Gordon Numns
Report No.	53	55	57	58	59
Date of reference	9 October 1973	21 June 1973	26 July 1973	24 January 1973	18 September 1973
Date of report	1 November 1973	21 December 1973	15 February 1974	13 March 1974	25 March 1974
Origin of reference	Employer application	Application by ALAE	Application by NUBE	Application by NUBE	Application by TUBE
Industry	Engineering	Air transport	Building society	Banking	Betting offices
Type of employee	White-collar and manual	Manual: mechanics and stock clerks	White-collar: managerial and clerical. Some manual ancillary staff.	White-collar: managerial and clerical	White-collar: supervisory and clerical
No. of employees covered by reference	66	176	186	4,584	18
Type of establishment	Single-establishment company	Multi-national company	Multi-establishment organisation	Multi-establishment company	Multi-establishment company
Description of employees in recommended unit(s)	Manual employees engaged in manufacture of edges and teeth for earthmoving equipment and stores employees	All mechanics and stock clerks employed by the company at Heathrow	1. Branch managers 2. All other staff except cleaners	All clerical, auxiliary and computer staff below the level of board-appointed staff	All betting office staff
No. in unit(s)	28	176	1. 16 2. 147	4,333	18
Recommended agent(s)	AUEW (Engineering section)	AUEW (TASS)	1. NUBE 2. NUBE	NUBE	TUBE
Other possible agents	None	ALAE	1. BBSBMA 2. BBSSA	BBSA	None

Reference	William Hill Organization	Seymour and Story Group	Airline Engineering Limited	The Associated Octel Company Limited	Davenport CB and Brewery Holdings Limited
Report No.	63	64	66	68	70
Date of reference	21 March 1973	11 October 1973	12 September 1973	18 May 1973	25 September 1973
Date of report	24 April 1974	23 April 1974	26 April 1974	9 May 1974	20 May 1974
Origin of reference	Application by TUBE	Application by TUBE	Application by ALAE	Application by the Secretary of State for Employment	Employer application
Industry	Betting offices	Betting offices	Aircraft maintenance	Petrochemicals	Brewing: bottling, distribution and sales
Type of employee	White-collar: supervisory and clerical	White-collar: supervisory and clerical	Manual: aircraft mechanics. White-collar: technical staff	White-collar: supervisory and work study	All employees: white-collar, production and maintenance
No. of employees covered by reference	3,514	165	42	171	1,450
Type of establishment	Multi-establishment company	Multi-establishment company	Single-establishment company	Multi-establishment company	Multi-establishment company
Description of employees in recommended unit(s)	All full-time and regular part-time staff at and below supervisory level in head offices and at and below the level of area supervisor in the licensed betting offices	No unit was recommended	No unit was recommended	All supervisors and MIOs at Ellesmere Port, Northwich and Amlwch	All brewery workers and draymen
No. in unit(s)	3,514	—	—	164	80
Recommended agent(s)	TUBE	No agent was recommended	No agent was recommended	ASTMS	TGWU
Other possible agents	None	Two staff committees	None	None	None

Reference	John Joyce Limited	Ken Hailes Limited	Messrs. Roland Jones	Ken Munden Limited	Temperance Permanent Building Society
Report No.	71	72	73	74	75
Date of reference	14 September 1973	26 October 1973	18 September 1973	18 September 1973	14 September 1973
Date of report	23 May 1974	23 May 1974	23 May 1974	23 May 1974	28 May 1974
Origin of reference	Application by TUBE	Application by TUBE	Application by TUBE	Application by TUBE	Application by NUBE
Industry	Betting offices	Betting offices	Betting offices	Betting offices	Building society
Type of employee	White-collar: supervisory and clerical	White-collar: supervisory and clerical	White-collar: supervisory and clerical	White-collar: supervisory and clerical	White-collar: managers and other supervisory and clerical staff
No. of employees covered by reference	104	36	34	194	464
Type of establishment	Multi-establishment company	Multi-establishment company	Multi-establishment company	Multi-establishment company	Multi-establishment organisation
Description of employees in recommended unit(s)	All full-time and part-time employees up to but not including senior managers	No unit was recommended	No unit was recommended	All full-time and regular part-time employees up to but not including area managers	No unit was recommended
No. in unit(s)	104	—	—	194	—
Recommended agent(s)	TUBE	No agent was recommended	No agent was recommended	TUBE	No agent was recommended
Other possible agents	None	None	None	None	None

Reference	The Anglia Building Society	Hector MacDonald Limited	Norwich Union Insurance Group
Report No.	79	81	82
Date of reference	13 September 1973	28 March 1974	20 March 1973
Date of report	23 July 1974	26 July 1974	30 July 1974
Origin of reference	Application by NUBE	Application by TUBE	Application by NUGSA
Industry	Building society	Betting offices	Insurance
Type of employee	White-collar: managerial, supervisory and clerical	White-collar: supervisory and clerical	White-collar: managerial, supervisory and clerical
No. of employees covered by reference	779	230	6,828
Type of establishment	Multi-establishment organisation	Multi-establishment company	Multi-establishment organisation
Description of employees in recommended unit(s)	No unit was recommended	No unit was recommended	No unit was recommended
No. in unit(s) *Recommended agent(s)*	— No agent was recommended	— No agent was recommended	— No agent was recommended
Other possible agents	ABSSA	None	ASTMS

Appendix II:
The views of the parties and CIR recommendations

Brief summaries of the views of the parties in references under Section 46 of the Act which we examined and the units recommended are set out below*:

(1) C. A. Parsons and Co. Limited and associated companies (CIR Report No. 32)

Company: Preference (by implication) for a unit for technicians below the line only.

TASS: Wished to retain exclusive bargaining rights for a unit below the line.

UKAPE: Wanted a bargaining unit incorporating qualified engineers above and below the line starting from the "new graduate level" of entry.

ASTMS: Wanted a unit for assistant managers and managers above the line and extending into other "Working Arrangements".

CIR: Recommended a unit below the line which accorded with the wishes of the company and TASS.

(2) Allied Breweries (UK) Limited (CIR Report No. 38)

Company: Wanted three separate bargaining units based on the "management companies".

TGWU: Wanted a separate unit for the "A, B and D" districts of Ansells.

NALHM: Wanted a single unit for the whole of Allied Breweries.

CIR: Recommended three separate units based on the "management companies". This accorded with the wishes of the company and tended to favour the views of TGWU rather than NALHM.

---

*Copies of the reports should be referred to for a fuller statement of these views.

(3) Coventry Economic Building Society (CIR Report No. 42)

Company: Probably favoured separate units for different levels of staff.

NUBE: Wanted one unit to cover all staff below senior management level.

CIR: Recommended one unit to cover all staff below senior management level. This accorded with the wishes of NUBE.

(4) Horizon Holidays Limited and associated companies (CIR Report No. 43)

Company: Wanted a unit to include all grades apart from senior managers in all locations of the companies.

ASTMS: Wanted a unit to include all grades apart from senior managers at the Acton office only.

CIR: Recommended a unit to include all grades apart from senior managers at the Acton office. This accorded with the wishes of ASTMS.

(5) Connor and Forbes Limited (CIR Report No. 44)

Company: No views recorded relating to the shape of unit(s).

LGSA: No views recorded relating to the shape of unit(s).

TUBE: Wanted a unit for all employees in the company except for casual employees.

CIR: Recommended a unit to cover all employees in the company up to and including area managers: full-time and regular part-time staff. This accorded with the wishes of TUBE.

(6) Con Mech (Engineers) Limited (CIR Report No. 53)

Company: Wanted a company-wide unit.

AUEW: Wanted to represent employees at Woking works employed on manual work below the level of foreman and chargehand in the earth-moving section and stores.

CIR: Recommended a unit to include employees at Woking works employed on manual work below the level of foreman and chargehand in the earth-moving section and stores. This accorded with the wishes of the AUEW.

(7) Pan American World Airways Incorporated (CIR Report No. 55)

Company: Wanted to maintain a single unit for all mechanics and stock clerks. A less-favoured alternative would consist of one unit comprising all aircraft and radio mechanics (licensed and unlicensed) and another for all other mechanics and stock clerks.

ALAE: Wanted a separate bargaining unit for licensed aircraft and radio mechanics.

AUEW: Wanted a unit for all mechanics and stock clerks.

CIR: Recommended a unit for all mechanics and stock clerks. This accorded with the wishes of the company and the AUEW.

(8) The Bridgwater Building Society (CIR Report No. 57)

Company: Expressed no clear preference regarding bargaining units but by implication wanted separate units for branch managers and the remainder of the staff.

BBSSA: Was prepared to accept a separate unit for branch managers.

BBSBMA: The members of this association wanted to retain separate negotiating arrangements from the rest of the staff.

NUBE: Was prepared to accept separate units for the branch managers and for the remainder of the staff.

CIR: Recommended one unit for the branch managers and a unit for the remainder of the staff. This was acceptable to all the parties.

(9) Barclays Bank International Limited (CIR Report No. 58)

Company: Wanted to continue with bargaining arrangements which were independent of those for Barclays Bank Limited. Was prepared to accept bargaining for board-appointed staff below the level of general managers assistant, provided the group constituted a separate bargaining unit. Would prefer the computer staff to be included in the same bargaining unit as clerical staff.

NUBE: Wanted to continue with bargaining arrangements which were independent of those for Barclays Bank Limited.

BBSA: Wanted a single bargaining unit covering the whole of the Barclays group. If the group unit were not to be conceded, BBSA would prefer a single unit for Barclays International with separate negotiations for the various groups of staff.

CIR:	Recommended one bargaining unit for non-board-appointed staff within Barclays International. This accorded with the wishes of NUBE and the company for arrangements which were separate from Barclays Bank Limited. It accorded with the preference of the company for incorporating computer staff in the same unit as clerical staff. No unit was recommended for board-appointed staff.

(10) Messrs. Gordon Nunns (CIR Report No. 59)

Company:	Was opposed to the principle of recognition.
TUBE:	Wanted a unit for all employees of Gordon Nunns.
CIR:	Recommended a unit comprising all betting shop staff employed by Gordon Nunns. This accorded with the wishes of TUBE.

(11) William Hill Organization (CIR Report No. 63)

Company:	Favoured a group-wide bargaining unit for all staff up to but not including area managers.
TUBE:	Wanted a group-wide bargaining unit for all staff up to but not including area managers.
CIR:	Recommended a group-wide bargaining unit for all staff up to but not including area managers. This accorded with the wishes of both parties.

(12) Seymour and Story Group (CIR Report No. 64)

Company:	Wanted separate bargaining units for the Lancashire and Yorkshire areas.
Staff Committees:	Wanted separate bargaining units for the Lancashire and Yorkshire areas.
TUBE:	Wanted a unit for all employees of the company up to but not including area managers.
CIR:	Was unable to make any recommendations due to lack of support for TUBE.

(13) Airline Engineering Limited (CIR Report No. 66)

Company:	Wanted to retain a unit including both aircraft engineers and technical back-up staff.
ALAE:	Wanted a bargaining unit containing only licensed aircraft engineers.

84

CIR:	Favoured a unit covering both licensed and unlicensed aircraft engineers but not technical back-up staff. The CIR was unable to make any recommendations because of ALAE's restrictive membership policy.

(14) The Associated OCTEL Company Limited (Second Report) (CIR Report No. 68)

Company:	Preferred a company-wide bargaining unit.
The Supervisory Forum:	Favoured a company-wide unit.
ASTMS:	Prepared to accept a company-wide unit but believed that Ellesmere Port alone would be a viable unit.
CIR:	Recommended a company-wide unit for supervisors and method improvement officers. This was acceptable to all parties.

(15) Davenport Brewery (Holdings) Limited (CIR Report No. 70)

Company:	Preferred a unit for all manual employees at the Bath Row site (this would include the bottling plant, the brewery, draymen and the distribution depot).
TGWU:	Wanted a unit for manual workers in the brewery, including the draymen.
CIR:	Recommended a unit covering the brewery and the draymen.

(16) John Joyce Limited (CIR Report No. 71)

Company:	Expressed reservations about the appropriateness of recognition.
TUBE:	Wanted a unit comprising all employees of the company.
CIR:	Recommended a company-wide unit for all full-time and regular part-time employees of the company. This was to include employees both in the betting shops and head office but to exclude those with senior managerial responsibilities. This would be acceptable to TUBE.

(17) Ken Hailes Limited (CIR Report No. 72)

Company:	Was opposed to recognition.
TUBE:	Wanted to represent all employees up to but not including the area manager.

CIR:	Was unable to make any recommendations because of inadequate support for TUBE.

(18) Messrs. Roland Jones (CIR Report No. 73)

Company:	Recognition not considered to be an urgent issue.
TUBE:	Wanted to represent all betting office employees.
CIR:	Was unable to make any recommendations because of inadequate support for TUBE.

(19) Ken Munden (Turf Accountant) Limited; Ken Munden (Racing) Limited (CIR Report No. 74)

Company:	Wanted the bargaining unit to include staff in both the Munden and Sherman's groups.
TUBE:	Wanted a bargaining unit to cover only staff in the Munden group.
CIR:	Recommended a unit to cover staff up to but not including area managers in the Munden group. This accorded with the wishes of TUBE.

(20) Temperance Permanent Building Society (CIR Report No. 75)

Company:	Wanted separate negotiations for the managers from the remainder of the staff.
NUBE:	Expressed no preference on the question of bargaining units.
CIR:	Distinguished between managers and other staff but was unable to make any recommendations due to lack of support for NUBE.

(21) Anglia Building Society (CIR Report No. 79)

Company:	Wanted a single bargaining unit for all staff.
ABSSA:	Wanted a unit for all staff.
NUBE:	Wanted either a separate bargaining unit for the data processing department and another for head office and the Northampton regional office *or* these two units with a third for all staff in branches outside of Northampton.
CIR:	Favoured a single unit for all staff but was unable to make any recommendations because the ABSSA was not independent and NUBE had inadequate support.

(22) Hector Macdonald Limited (CIR Report No. 81)

Company: Was opposed to recognition.

TUBE: Wanted to represent all employees up to but not including area managers.

CIR: Made no recommendations because of inadequate support for TUBE.

(23) Norwich Union Insurance Group (CIR Report No. 82)

Company: Wished to negotiate with a single bargaining agent.

NUGSA: Was prepared to accept a group-wide unit.

ASTMS: Was prepared to accept a group-wide unit.

CIR: Made no formal recommendations.

Appendix III:
List of abbreviations

ABSSA	Anglia Building Society Staff Association
ACTS	Association of Clerical, Technical and Supervisory Staffs
ALAE	Association of Licensed Aircraft Engineers
AMRCSTS	Association of the Medical Research Council Scientific and Technical Staff
APST	Association of Professional Scientists and Technologists
ASEE	Association of Supervisory and Executive Engineers
ASTMS	Association of Scientific, Technical and Managerial Staffs
AUEW	Amalgamated Union of Engineering Workers
AUT	Association of University Teachers
BBSA	Barclays Bank Staff Association
BBSBMA	Bridgwater Building Society Branch Managers' Association
BBSSA	Bridgwater Building Society Staff Association
BMA	British Medical Association
CAWU	Clerical and Administrative Workers' Union
CUGSA	Commercial Union Group Staff Association
EEF	Engineering Employers' Federation
EETU/PTU	Electrical, Electronic Telecommunication and Plumbing Trades Union
GMWU	General and Municipal Workers' Union
LGSA	Leisure and General Staff Association
MRC	Medical Research Council
NALHM	National Association of Licensed House Managers
NUBE	National Union of Bank Employees
NUFTO	National Union Furniture Trade Operatives
NUGSA	Norwich Union Group Staff Association
SAGA	Staff Association—General Accident
TASS	Technical and Supervisory Section of AUEW
TGWU	Transport and General Workers' Union
TUBE	The Union of Bookmakers' Employees
UIS	Union of Insurance Staffs
UKAPE	United Kingdom Association of Professional Engineers
USDAW	Union of Shop, Distributive and Allied Workers

List of Commission's reports

Available from H.M.S.O. bookshops in London (49 High Holborn WC1V 6HB or by post from P.O. Box 569, London SE1 9NH), Edinburgh, Cardiff, Belfast, Manchester, Bristol and Birmingham or through booksellers.

Report No.		Price	Price by Post
1	The Associated Octel Company Limited	10p	13p
2	General Accident Fire and Life Assurance Corporation Limited	10p	13p
3	W. Stevenson and Sons, Suttons Cornwall Limited	10p	13p
4	Birmid Qualcast	25p	29p
5	BSR Limited	15p	18p
6	Elliots of Newbury Limited	11p	14p
7	Brocks Fireworks Limited	10p	13p
8	Frederick Parker Limited	11p	14p
9	First General Report	18½p	21½p
10	International Harvester Co. of Great Britain Limited	24p	27p
11	Hoover Limited	35p	39p
12	Medical Research Council	22½p	25½p
13	Armstrong Patents Co. Limited	20p	23p
14	Standard Telephones and Cables Limited	30p	34p
15	Clayton Dewandre Co. Limited	30p	34p
16	Commercial Union Assurance Co. Limited	24p	27p
17	Facilities afforded to shop stewards	40p	44p
18	Electrolux Limited	30p	34p
19	Scottish Stamping and Engineering Limited	25p	29p
20	Joseph Lucas Limited	45p	49p
21	Electric Windings (London) Limited	12½p	15½p
22	Shipbuilding and shiprepairing	£1·15p	£1·23p
23	The Hotel and Catering Industry Part I. Hotels and Restaurants	45p	49p
24	British Home Stores	22½p	25½p
25	Second General Report	24p	27p
26	Engelhard Industries Limited	35p	39p
27	The Hotel and Catering Industry Part II. Industrial Catering	37½p	41½p
28	John Bamber Engineering Limited	25p	29p
29	Alcan Smelter Site	50p	55½p
30	Approved Closed Shop Agreement British Shipping Federation/National Union of Seamen	35p	39p
31	Disclosure of information	45p	49p
32	C. A. Parsons & Co. Limited and associated companies	35p	39p
33	Industrial relations training	75p	80½p
33A	Industrial relations training (statistical supplement)	£1·25p	£1·35p
34	The role of management in industrial relations	38p	42p
35	Williams and Glyn's Bank Limited	30p	34p
36	The Hotel and Catering Industry Part III. Public houses, clubs and other sectors	50p	55½p
37	Annual report for 1972	40p	44p
38	Allied Breweries (UK) Limited	35p	39p
39	Communications and collective bargaining	35p	39p
40	Approved closed shop in theatre, independent television and films	50p	55½p
41	National Coal Board Bulk Terminal, Immingham	20p	23p
42	Coventry Economic Building Society	28p	32p
43	Horizon Holidays Limited and associated companies	35p	39p
44	Connor and Forbes Limited	25p	29p
45	Walter Alexander and Company (Coachbuilders) Limited	40p	44p
46	Coffin Furniture and Cerement-making Wages Council	35p	39p
47	Hollow-ware Wages Council	38p	42p
48	Keg and Drum Wages Council	38p	42p
49	Pin, Hook and Eye and Snap Fastener Wages Council	40p	44p
50	Stamped or Pressed Metal-Wares Wages Council	38p	42p
51	Boot and Floor Polish Wages Council (Great Britain)	25p	29p
52	General Accident Fire and Life Assurance Corporation Limited (Second Report)	40p	44p
53	Con-Mech (Engineers) Limited	15p	18p

Commission on Industrial Relations, 140 Gower Street, London WC1E 6HT. Tel: 01-387 4333

Printed in England for Her Majesty's Stationery Office by Burrup, Mathieson & Co., Ltd. London SE1 0NX.   S701129 CH   Dd 288550 K32 8/74